UniverseSoul

UniverseSoul

Stephen Safer

Harvester of Sparks Publishing

Dedication

To all the warrior souls.

Contents

Acknowledgements

All thanks and praise to the Infinite for everything. It is with profound gratitude to Hashem that I present this book.

I'd also like to express deep appreciation to Ohr Somayach in Monsey, NY, Aish HaTorah in Jerusalem, Rabbi Yosef Edelstein, Rabbi Naftali Reich, Rabbi Aaron Garfinkel, my esteemed uncle – Rabbi Avraham Yaakov Finkel ז״ל (for the inspiration), Chaim Rabhan, Shlomy Slatus, Michael Snaid, Janie & Brad Cherney, Joey Rosen & Lizzie Daiss (at Creative Approach) for book cover assistance, Dan Weinstein, Rabbi Ephraim Rabhan, Rabbi Avigdor and Rebbetzin Rochel Slatus, Edward Rabhan (for diligence in putting together the Divrei Torah publication in Savannah, GA), and the entire Congregation Bnai Brith Jacob (BBJ) Synagogue in Savannah, where many of these writings were first published in the weekly Divrei Torah over the years.

To my dearly respected and treasured in-laws: HaRav Gavriel Finkel זצ״ל (Zaidy), Rebbetzin Miriam Finkel (Bubby) and the mishpacha for their ongoing encouragement and guidance.

Finally, thank you to my extraordinary wife, Shifra and our dear children – Shai, Esther & Nitzevet. You all make me a better person, a better Jew. May Hashem grant us extended years of health, shefa, shalom, nachas and bracha.

Introduction

Building and expanding on my first book, *The Infinity Frequency,* portions of *UniverseSoul* have been garnered from great rabbis, mystics, teachers and thinkers. Every so often, I try to convey esoteric principles that I admittedly have a limited scope of in breadth and depth. I do so because I know the time is short. Our lives are lived on the brink in blinks.

I have a penchant for writing and coloring with words. Especially about concepts that are thought provoking and spiritual. Ideas that are a departure from the norm and stretch the mind are most appealing.

I'm not a scholar and far from intellectual in its strictest sense. I frequently quote and write about what moves or speaks to me. I don't often put things together from a scholarly angle. The articles offered here are mainly psychospiritual in nature with Judaic tones.

In brief, I write for Light. Writing for me is more about expression than perfection. I just want to share what I have learned, heard, read or an idea that crossed my mind in order to spread some light and perspective. I'm simply trying to remain creative, positive and grateful with the time I'm allotted.

It is my ardent hope that the essays included within these pages will reach the essence of the reader, spark inspiration and arouse a deeper sense of meaning and well-being, while simultaneously being interesting & entertaining.

There's something quite intimate about reading someone's thoughts & feelings in written form. To be granted access to the mind quietly, in an uninterrupted fashion with words is so special. What one authorizes to pass through the "gates" is personal. Thank you for your time and for allowing me to enter.

I once heard: Sleep doesn't help if it's your soul that's tired. I know some of you are tired, but please, come this way...

Prologue

The paradox of our time in history is that we have taller buildings, but shorter tempers; wider freeways, but narrower viewpoints. We spend more, but have less. We buy more, but enjoy less. We have bigger houses, but less room. More conveniences, but less time. We have more degrees, but less sense; more knowledge, but less judgment. More experts, yet more problems; more medicine, but less wellness. We drink too much, smoke too much, spend too recklessly, laugh too little, drive too fast, get too angry, stay up too late, get up too tired, read too little, watch TV too much and pray too seldom. We have multiplied our possessions, but reduced our values. We talk too much, love too seldom, and hate too often. We've learned how to make a living, but not a life. We have the means to live, but no meaning to live for. We've added years to life, but not life to years. We've been all the way to the moon and back, but have trouble crossing the street to meet a new neighbor. We conquered outer space, but not inner space. We've done larger things, but not better things. We've cleaned up the air, but polluted the soul. We've conquered the atom, but not our prejudice. We write more, but learn less. We plan more, but accomplish less. We've learned to rush, but not to wait. We build more computers and phones to hold more information, but we communicate less and less. These are the times of fast foods and slow digestion; big men and small character. Steep profits and shallow relationships. These are the days of two incomes, but more divorce. Fancier houses, but broken homes. These are days of quick trips, disposable diapers, throwaway morality, one night stands, and pills that do everything from cheer, to quiet, to kill. It is a time when there is much in the showroom window and nothing in the stockroom. So please, take stock… Remember to spend some time with your loved ones because they are not going to be around forever. Remember, say a kind word to someone who looks up to you because that little person soon will grow up and leave your side. Remember to say, 'I love you' to your loved ones; and most of all mean it. Remember, cherish the moment for someday that person will not be there again. Never take anyone for granted because you might wake up one day and realize you lost a diamond while you were busy collecting stones. Give time to love, speak, listen and share. And always remember, life is not measured by the number of breaths we take, but by those moments that take our breath away. – Unknown

---

For all souls are really one. Only the body divides us.
Behold, Hashem is the soul of the universe.

1

Apocalyptic Statistic

"Anything that annoys you is teaching you patience. Anyone who abandons you is teaching you how to stand on your own two feet. Anything that angers you is teaching you forgiveness & compassion. Anything that has power over you is teaching you how to take the power back. Anything you hate is teaching you unconditional love. Anything you fear is teaching you courage to overcome your fear. Anything you can't control is teaching you how to let go." When we don't learn these lessons, we lessen our learning. We diminish our ability to balance and walk the wire of life.

The unseating of equanimity is a severance of balance and symmetry. Rabbi Freifeld, zt"l, would talk about the contours of a person. The dimensions and parameters of the human being, and learning to align with the symmetry of the universe. To be in contact, in touch with eternity. To be a human being, he taught, is to be a human becoming. The ability to become more than the past and present self.

Continuously and consciously working to reside in universal symmetry and balance with the Oneness. With proper inculcation of the aforementioned, we now stand more poised and composed as to not upset the delicate physical, psychological and spiritual landscapes/soulscapes of our lives.

While others continue to defiantly marinate in their own prejudices and parade their arrogant and irrational, vituperative responses, we have a rich opportunity to use this time to seek inner peace and personal growth. Yet, as Rabbi Freeman states, "Prisoners. We are all prisoners. But we sit on the keys. Finitude is our cell. The universe is our prison. Our jail keeper is the Act of Being. The keys to liberation are clenched tightly in the fists of our own ego." Ergo, let's go let go of our ego. Let go, or be dragged.

If you're blaming everything and everyone else for your problems that's part of your problem. Much of the anger and impatience exhibited is related to selfishness and ego. Indeed, your level of anger and irritability can often be linked proportionally to your level of ego. To overcome the outer world, overcome your inner self.

The Chazon Ish said, "Certainty is a matter of trust that there is no coincidence in the world; everything that happens is divinely orchestrated." A symphonic, symmetrical, symbiotic arrangement.

Introspection or extrospection? Have you become an apocalyptic statistic? Have you become a *numb*er? Has the world got you whirled, spinning and teetering on the edge?

Are you trying to run away from it all on a so called apocalyptical elliptical and going nowhere?

Exercise with tenacity. Seek balance.

Become. Come be. For the stronger you become, the gentler you will be.

Know, "This world is like a mountain. Your echo depends on you. If you scream good things, the world will give it back. If you scream bad things, the world will give it back. Even if someone says badly about you, speak well about him. Change your heart to change the world. Your task is not to seek for love, but merely to seek and find all the barriers within yourself that you have built against it."

It's been said, "Your life does not get better by chance, it gets better by change." Some people want to see things change, but are unwilling to change things in themselves. The beginning of change is at the end of the comfort zone.

Our biggest battles are not with other people or other countries, it's the war within. Don't become a casualty of all that you see and hear. It's been conveyed, "some people are waiting for a final apocalyptic war. But the final war is fought not on battlefields, nor at sea, nor in the skies above. Neither is it a war between leaders or nations. The final war is fought in the heart of each human being, with the armies of his or her deeds in this world." The Talmud relates, Man has three friends on whose company he relies. First, wealth which goes with him only while good fortune lasts. Second, his relatives; they go only as far as the grave and leave him there. The third friend, his good deeds, go with him far beyond the grave.

After all is said and done, it's better to have done than said. "X" the excuses. Start making uses. An insightful person stated, "Rationalization is a process of not perceiving reality, but of attempting to make reality fit one's emotions." Take note, *rationalize* can be read & said as ration-lies; the rationing of lies. As in collecting, be*lie*ving and feeding off of the lies, distortions, emotional fabrications and falsifications.

The Baal Shem Tov taught that balance means responding to criticism and applause in the same ways — not to be controlled to either.

I once asked a wise person, "could you please tell me what field would make a great career?" He replied with a smile, "work to be a good human being. There is a lot of opportunity in this area and very little competition."

Work to live in symmetry and strive for equanimity. We should all try to make peace with life's difficulties inside ourselves, that way we are better equipped to handle life's difficulties outside ourselves. In doing so, we deflate the doomed apocalyptic, negativistic outlook and inflate the equanimous input. Thereby putting an end to the protracted "error" of pessimism and transforming an ill-fated apocalypse into an epoch-alypse of harmony and good will.

2

Ctrl Alt Del

Ctrl Alt Del = Ctrl – control yourself. Alt – alter your thoughts. Del – delete negativity.

In the pursuit of stability when we learn to cope there is often hope. However, if we're cope-less we're apt to feel hopeless. This is your choice: A brave new world or a grave new world? Humility, courage and discipline are pivotal to coping and the unveiling of your true self. Change how you see and see how you change.

"Finding yourself" is not really how it works. You aren't a ten-dollar bill in last winter's coat pocket. You are also not lost. Your true self is right there, buried under cultural conditioning, other people's opinions, and inaccurate conclusions you drew as a kid that became your beliefs about who you are. "Finding yourself" is actually returning to yourself. An unlearning, an excavation, a remembering who you were before the world got its hands on you," wrote E. McDowell.

Go forth and learn. Ctrl Alt Del.

In the words of Rav Avigdor Miller, this is the way of many people, they busy themselves with garnering as many sensations and momentary temporary pleasures as possible: movies, television, theatre, newspapers, art and everything and anything they can shove down their (eyes, ears and) throats, the more the better. However, our love can be dedicated to preparation. The foundations of belief are that we can transcend the physical world by elevating it and connecting it all back to its root Source. The less emphasis on material attachments below, the better the spiritual connection above.

Pursue the science of faith. Trust the process. "Everyone who is seriously involved in the pursuit of science becomes convinced that a spirit is manifest in the laws of the universe – a spirit vastly superior to that of man, and one in the face of which we with our modest powers must feel humble," shared A. Einstein. He continues, "If you want different results, do not do the same things."

It's your responsibility and your response-ability that sculpts your life. In perpetuity we seek wisdom while simultaneously manifesting positive actions. The Rambam said, "We each decide whether to make ourselves learned or ignorant, compassionate or cruel, generous or miserly. No one forces us. No one decides for us. We are responsible for what we are." Keep in mind that your value doesn't decrease based on someone's inability to see your worth.

Content people construct their inner world. Discontent

people blame their outer world. If you focus on the hurt, you will continue to suffer. If you focus on the lesson, you will continue to grow.

Moreover, Solomon Ibn Gavriel taught, "Man is wise only while in search of wisdom; when he imagines he has attained it, he is a fool." The Talmud relates, A person whose wisdom exceeds his good deeds is likened to a tree whose branches are numerous, but whose roots are few. The wind comes and uproots it and turns it upside down. But, a person whose good deeds exceed his wisdom is likened to a tree whose branches are few but whose roots are numerous. Even if all the winds of the world were to come and blow against it, they could not budge it from its place. The leaves may change but the roots remain. As it's been said, "We cannot direct the wind, but we can adjust the sails."

We can control ourselves, alter our thoughts and delete negativity by also understanding Rav Pinson's words, "Each individual experiences life in two worlds. There is the outer world and there is the inner world. One is the realm of the effect while the other is the realm of the cause. When we surrender to the sensory impressions of the outer world, then life is in the realm of effect, and we continually find ourselves in situations and predicaments that feel beyond our control. However, if we live from the inside out, we then live as masters. The interior, inner world, is the essence and the cause of the outer."

Your path home is not outside; it's inside.

Stop sacrificing your thoughts on the altar of negativity

and alter your thoughts to positivity & sanguinity then things will begin to change. Halt pressing retrieve on things that should be deleted. Ctrl Alt Del. It's time to restart from the inside out by creating light filled, life affirming algorithms. Let's push the keys on the board of life in unison to reboot a higher unity. A global, collective conscience of Oneness, positivity and possibility.

3

Manufacturers of Hope

"There was never a night or a problem that could defeat a sunrise or hope."

For a moment let's stop "what if'ing," and catastrophizing everything including stress and the overemphasis that society places on money, job, status, media, politicization and the like. Many spend their lives in constant worry, fury and conflict over such things. The material outweighing what's truly meaningful and purposeful. Hope is scarce on such faces and in such places. Often their mercurial temperaments are exposed by not having full control. The benighted souls are left with blighted hopes. It's been conveyed, "Now that your worry has proved such an unlucrative business, why not find a better job?" Worrying does not take away tomorrow's troubles. It takes away today's peace.

When we don't have our external expectations met repeatedly, we occasionally lose hope. Placing our hopes exclusively in "man" or physical things leaves one diluted and disappointed. This is abundantly clear during these trying times. A negative mind will not create a positive life. By the way, life is under no obligation to give us what we expect or think we deserve. "Hope is seeing light despite being surrounded by darkness."

What if we stopped "what if'ing?" It is the perpetual, amplified anxiety question of "what if" that leaves a bitter aftertaste and the lingering vapors of fear and hopelessness. Many "what ifs" never even materialize or come to be. And nevertheless, so many spend their lives right there in its wretched, dispirited grips. These quivering jowls of uncertainty certainly siphon hope. So, instead let's replace "what if" with "what now?" What can you do now? Open a can of "can." Drink from it. "Look past your thoughts, so you may drink the pure nectar of this moment." Right now, as you read this hopefully you're present and mindful in the moment because even if you have perceivably lost "everything" you've lost nothing if you have a glimmer of hope. Please let your hopes, not your hurts shape your future. This brand of hope can be born from within. It takes seeking something more meaningful than just the physical pleasures. It takes work. We must sometimes have the intestinal fortitude to create our own inspiration and hope from deep inside ourselves; to become a hope factory of sorts. Working in this anti-pollutant industry requires ingenuity, strength and wisdom. Note too, "there is no better exercise for your heart than reaching down and helping to lift someone up."

By generating a small spark of hope from within we can

gradually stoke those embers of light into something greater. A mystic said, "It's good to leave each day behind, like flowing water, free of sadness. Yesterday is gone and its tale told. Today new seeds are growing. Your mind is a garden. Your thoughts are the seeds. You can grow flowers or you can grow weeds."

Just because you feel negative doesn't mean you have to think negative. Mental and spiritual health 101 is about finding positive things to do with your negative thoughts and feelings. It's been expressed, "Every wall is a door." Don't overestimate your problems, and underestimate yourself.

Practice optimism. Manifest it.

Happiness is letting go of what you assume your life should be like right now, and sincerely appreciating it for everything that it is. So, relax. You are enough. You have enough. You do enough. Release, and live right now in this very moment. Consider this, "If you miss the present moment, you miss your appointment with life." Look for the positive and you will see the positive. Switch your inner dialogue and mentality from, "I'm broken & helpless" to, "I'm growing & healing" and watch how your life gradually changes for the better.

A wise rabbi said, "In every hardship, search for the spark of good and cling to it. The greater the hardship, the more wondrous the good it bears. If you cannot find that good, rejoice that wonder beyond your comprehension has befallen you. Embrace that wonder and it will open itself to you."

You won the lottery! It's called life. Now, how are you going to spend it?!

In the radiant words of Anne Frank, "What a wonderful thought it is that some of the best days of our lives haven't even happened yet" and "How wonderful it is that nobody need wait a single moment before beginning to improve the world." The healing rays of hope thrive on such expressions. Thus, budget your time and learn to spend your energy wisely.

Rabbi Rome imparts from the Baal HaTanya that mystically speaking there's a concept of "plowing" our inner field by preparing our minds and hearts for planting. We must "plow" and uproot the negative to plant new, positive, redemptive seeds. We are preparing our minds to plant new ideas. We want those seeds planted in fertile ground. So, by "plowing" and uprooting the so-called weeds and stones we are loosening up the hard and stubborn soil/earth, the rigid mentality; we're loosening our attachments, recalcitrance and ego. By getting rid of all those "weeds and stones" we remove the blockages that may have prevented the new seeds from taking root. As such, we're prepared to plant and bring hopeful, growth-oriented seeds of positive change.

If you strive to see the positive side(s) of everything you'll live a richer life than many.

You're not alone. We're all in this together; "do not feel lonely, the entire universe is inside you." We don't wear the same shoes, but we share some of the same footprints. Don't carry your mistakes around with you. Instead, place them below your feet and use them as stepping stones to learn, grow and rise above. Fret not, hope is on the horizon. It may be a slow process, but quitting won't speed it up.

Please accept this offering, "I wish I could show you when you are lonely or in darkness, the astonishing light of your own being." I don't know who needs to hear this, but you're going to be ok.

If you don't take everything so personally, then personally everything won't take you.

Hope should not be contingent upon the physical, material (possessions) or another person per se. It is nestled in you as an individual and linked to something far more transcendental. It's made there. Seek it. Find it. Don't lose it. Use it. You too can become a manufacturer of hope. Now is the time. Here is the place. You are just the right person.

4

20/20

Well, 2020 is turning out to be quite the year. The manifestation of unyielding events, daunting. The signs and "mess"ages, a sting to the eyes. The unfolding scenarios may be making those who lack authentic faith &/or a spiritual framework increasingly more depressed and anxious.

How's your outer and inner visual acuity? When life gets blurry adjust your focus. Turn off the te*lie*vision to improve the tell-*truth*-vision. Now see and hear this: Many like to sit back and be entertained. Few like to stand up and make a change. "Life has no remote. Get up and change it yourself." Stop the mindless "scrolling" on the phone and start the mindful "scrolling" with the Torah; the one scroll prescribed for optimal vision.

Rabbi Freeman relates, The Zohar tells that there is a lower world—our world—and there is a higher world. Our world must continuously receive from that higher world. But how it receives depends upon our state of mind. If we glow with joy and vitality, then that higher world as well shines upon us in full glory and brings forth shefa (abundance). But if we wallow in depression and anxiety, then we can receive only the metered trickle that squeezes through such a constricted channel. Pessimism—damages the channels of blessing from Above. That is why King David said, "Serve G-d with joy!" Because your joy here draws upon you another joy from above. Frame it with the eyes of emunah (faith) and see it all from a fresh perspective.

Try a smile. A smile is expansive both facially and socially. It generates connectivity and positivity. An external smile creates internal cheer to both the giver and the recipient. It's contagious.

Rabbi Noach Weinberg shared, "It is a greater pleasure to love than to be loved. So why spend so much energy on gaining the approval of others? Work on loving them instead." Furthermore, when you feel that great surge of love within you should try to connect that deep, amplified feeling to Hashem. As it says, "To love Hashem with all your heart and soul."

Helen Keller said, "Although the world is full of suffering, it is also full of the overcoming of it. Optimism is the faith that leads to achievement. Nothing can be done without hope and confidence."

Instead of, "seeing is believing," Rebbe Nachman taught that, "believing is seeing!" As one's faith becomes a person's "eyes" by which one's life and vision comes into focus. One's outlook can assist in determining the outcome. Much of it depends on how you frame it.

See, the ultimate objective of spirituality is not to remove the existence of evil or humanity's negative traits. Instead, we must confront and transform these dark forces, for it is only through the struggle of transformation that we ignite the spark of divinity within us, wrote Rabbi Shimon bar Yochai. It's about cultivating awareness and revealing the unity of Hashem in the world.

Life is fragile. Handle with care & prayer. So, "Pray that you will never have to bear all that you are able to endure."

They say hindsight is 20/20. We need not look back for clarity. Focus now. Don't cheat on the present with the past. Take heed, "Courage does not always roar. Sometimes courage is the quiet voice at the end of the day saying I will try again tomorrow." Don't give up and in.

Some are rushing to get out of 2020 only to take the same thinking and behaviors into 2021.

A simple lesson can be learned in nature from a turtle. In order for the turtle to live, eat and move it must come out its shell. We too, must be willing to come out of our "shells" to move, adapt, change and grow.

A little PMA (positive mental attitude) helps keep the negativity at bay. Picture this: "Imagine you could open your eyes to see the good in every person, the positive in every circumstance, and the opportunity in every challenge."

This year has taught us more about faith, gratitude, humility, patience and kindness. May every year be filled with positive thoughts, kind deeds, and meaningful moments.

Clarity affords focus. If you look with the eyes of faith things will become clearer. The bleak, brighter; the blurred, crisper. Then you'll see, it's not totally about what the year did to you, but rather what you did in the year. A new year won't change your life. But new thoughts & better decisions will. It's less about how the year manages you. It's more about how you manage the year. Real 20/20 vision in 2020 and beyond.

5

Emunah Matters

"Who's more foolish, the child afraid of the dark or the adult afraid of the light?"

Step out of the dark and into the light.

Know, there's not one thing out of place. It's all right on time. Everything is providentially lighting the way to redemption. Fret not. As it's been said, "Faith it til you make it." Raise your voice. Rise up! Defeat the rat-race-ism.

The Zohar reveals that reality resembles a mirror. Every deed we perform, each emotion we display and every word we speak is reflected back to our lives in equal measure. Midah keneged midah/measure for measure.

Rav Ashlag (Baal HaSulam) imparted, "After being born in our world, one is obliged to change his heart from egoistic to altruistic, while living in this world. This is the purpose of his life, the reason behind his appearance in this world, and it is the goal of all creation. A complete replacement of egoistic desires with altruistic ones is called "gmar tikkun" (final rectification). Every individual and all of humanity must attain it in this world together."

From ego to we-go into this together. As wisely stated by the Ibn Ezra, "There is no greater poverty than ignorance." If so, many are poverty stricken. It's evident we all have much work to do. Let's accelerate compassion and put the brakes on hate. Bring the strength and light of faith & prayer to the forefront. Positive activism and prayer are healthy pathways to change.

Rabbi Moshe Chaim Luzzatto shared in Path of the Just, "Most precious of all is the practice of hisbodedus, solitude (meditation/prayer). For when a person removes worldly affairs from before his eyes, he removes their attraction from his heart. King David spoke in praise of hisbodedus when he said, "If only I had wings like a dove! Then I would fly away and be at rest. I would wander far off, I would lodge in the wilderness, I would hurry to a shelter from the raging wind and storm" (Psalms 55:7-8). We find that the prophets Elijah and Elisha had their own special place in the mountains for secluded prayer and meditation. The early sages and saints followed the same pathway, finding hitbodedut the best way to attain a state of complete detachment from the mundane world in order that vanities of their contemporaries should not cause them to waste their lives away."

If you're not working on yourself then you'll be worked on/up by everyone else. And, a wise aggadic elucidation should be taken to heart that the person capable of deceiving himself is far more dangerous than the person only deceiving others.

Pro-test or con-test, "Our lives are fashioned by our choices. First, we make our choices. Then, our choices make us."

We are put on the same planet, but we can choose the world we live in. Choose faith.

You may make mistakes. But remember, mistakes don't make you. Emunah (faith) perspective: It's not happening to me. It's happening for me.

Do what is right and Hashem will do what is left.

Fight to stay positive. Fight for your life with all of your light. There's nothing more powerful than a humble person with a warrior spirit driven by a higher purpose. A little faith banishes a lot of doubt. An indomitable emunah provides a light by which the darkness abates. Feed your faith and your fear will starve. It's been stated, "Faith is the strength by which a shattered world shall emerge into light. Hand in hand, intelligence and faith, understanding and wisdom, find their way into the most inner chambers of truth. Intelligence makes the journey; faith kicks down the door."

Start right here: Worry ends where emunah begins. Faith is not knowing what the future holds, but knowing Who holds the future.

Faith is not just a noun. It's a verb. Put it into action. Live it. Fertilize the ill-omened with the light of faith, peace, positivity and prayer. Arm in arm we can disarm the negativity. Faith is stability in an unstable world. Life matters.

You matter. Calm the riotous rifts within. Lament no more.
Emunah matters.

6

Supernatural

"We didn't come into this world to be natural. We came into this world to be supernatural."

We all struggle. It's natural. It's woven into the pattern of existence. Some quietly, others more noisily. Nevertheless, have heart, for stars are born in the dark and darkness dies in the light.

Willing to go beyond our animalistic nature authorizes an opportunity in which we can outshine our former "self" and become more (by refining our sefirotic/character traits in emulation of the Creator). Einstein added, "I must be willing to give up what I am in order to become what I will be." Transformation takes a measure of surrendering and courageously approaching new information with the sincere intent of implementation.

Rav Kook beautifully revealed, "The greater you are, the more you need to search for yourself. Your deep soul hides itself from consciousness. So, you need to increase elevation

of thinking, penetration of thought, liberation of mind —
until finally your soul reveals itself to you, spangling a few
sparkles of her lights. Then you find bliss, transcending all
humiliations or anything that happens, by attaining
equanimity, by becoming one with everything that happens,
by reducing yourself so extremely that you nullify your
individual, imaginary form, that you nullify existence in the
depth of your self. "What are we?" Then you know every
spark of truth, every bolt of integrity flashing anywhere.
Then you gather everything, without hatred, jealousy, or
rivalry. The light of peace and a fierce boldness manifest in
you. The desire to act and work, the passion to create and
to restore yourself, the yearning for silence and for the inner
shout of joy — these all band together in your spirit, and you
become holy." Holy in the sense of being distinct, unique,
separate from the profane and stretching beyond scientific
consensus and understanding, or the laws of our base nature
by which we're so often indentured.

In our instant gratification society prolonging gratification
may seem farfetched. However, prolonging gratification is
where the supernatural seedlings of change take root and see
fruition. We're planted in this world to grow. Just as the
seed has all its potential locked inside it, so too each of us
has unlocked potential. Like the seed, we must be willing to
push through the darkness, to break the through the surface
and reach for the sky. Through this process — growth mode
acceleration is activated by prolonging our lower level ego
gratification for something greater.

We've all heard, "you can't teach an old dog new tricks" &/or "I am the way I am; I'm set in my ways." I beg to differ. You can teach an old dog new tricks. It's not easy, but you can change. Society has poisoned and brain washed many to believe that they can't change. That's been the septic false narrative they shoved down our throats. Society sold it and many bought it. So, we remain caged and locked in our "ways." Never trying, hiding behind a legion of excuses and fear for not changing and going beyond our so-called nature. Change is possible. By the way, "When someone says, "you've changed" it simply means that you've stopped living your life their way."

Understand, complacency breeds mediocrity.

Stop stopping and start starting!

A wise rabbi related, in a sense, we have all wandered away from our true selves. Birth is the beginning of our soul's journey, sent off from its divine source to live in an unnatural state, a land of materialism. Throughout our lives, therefore, we crave to be reunited with our real selves. We search for our soul, for the G-dly spark within ourselves. We long to reconnect with our Source.

It's all Ain Sof (Infinite One). Everything you do and everywhere you go, you are constantly in the presence of G-d. Hashem permeates all of creation and beyond. Just because you don't perceive it or "feel" connected to G-d doesn't negate that spiritual reality. G-d is right here, right now. At any time you can tap into and access the light of the Essence. Pause and ponder. Think intently about this. If you truly work to intergrate this level of keen awareness into your being it will literally change your life. It will reorient how you think, speak and act, imparted Rabbi Rome.

Rebbe Nachman of Breslov was quoted as saying, "The day you were born is the day G-d decided the world could not exist without you." So, let your light shine so brightly that others can see their way out of the darkness. The Midrash says, "G-d always provides what we need, but we must be ready to open our eyes and see it."

A mystic poet said, "Knock, and He'll open the door. Vanish, and He'll make you shine like the sun. Fall, and He'll raise you to the heavens. Become nothing, and He'll turn you into everything."

Uplift. Find the nes (miracle) in every nisayon (test).

Live as if life is a miracle and everyday is a gift.

Our goal should be to live life in radical amazement. Get up in the morning and look at the world in a way that takes nothing for granted. Everything is phenomenal; everything is incredible; never treat life casually. To be spiritual is to be amazed, conveyed Rabbi Heschel.

Chazal related, "Ein davar ha'omeid bifnei haratzon," that is, "Nothing can stand in the way of the will." Will it into existence. The next level of your life will demand a different version of you. "Be the change you want to see in the world." Arise. Expand the borders. Elevate nature & the natural in order to grow, to become something more, something greater, something supernatural!

7

Gratitude Rx XR

A daily dose of gratitude is strongly recommended. Notice: Be aware; as it may cause severe shifts in perspective. May cause increased feelings of abundance and decreased feelings of fear, anxiety and agitation. May enhance awareness, and cause extreme awakening & wellbeing. Assists in operating the "heavy" machinery of life. There are unlimited refills on this prescription. Other side effects may include, but are not limited to: learning to count your blessings and making your blessings count.

Age and maturity often allows for a more robust, richer understanding of life. We compile memories all along the way. We engage in the pleasurable (albeit healthy &/or unhealthy) and attempt to disengage/avoid the painful. Markedly, we have arrived at so called "adulthood" to varying degrees; each according to his or her own innate perspicacity. We occasionally gain fresh perspectives and begin to shape our lives accordingly. Included, but not limited in this process is: autonomy, career, making friends, building and maintaining meaningful relationships, experiencing the delight of life and tolerating the agony of it as well.

However, somewhere along this life/timeline something gets lost. Something that once sparkled begins to fade. Life takes its toll. We grow, sometimes down and sometimes out. Jaded, we forget to breathe and the once vivified vapors of our being get siphoned by undesirable circumstances. As a resultant we disregard kindness and cultivate abuse in its many forms. We become so centered on the "I" we lose the meaning. Consequently, some problems become pro-blames. This is where we must garner and muster all of our mental and soulful fortitude. "Do not dwell in the well of unwellness." A steady dose of gratitude is called for in such times.

You are living and breathing right now as you read this… or are you? In a sense we are all on life-support from a higher Source. Mercy and faith is the air we breathe.

"G-d gave you a gift of 86,400 seconds today. Have you used one of them to say thank you." What oxygen is to the lungs, such is hope to the meaning of life, said R.W. Emerson. Gratitude is an appropriate prescription with a hopeful prognosis.

Time moves forward, but people sometimes don't. Breathe. Permit gratitude to penetrate every fiber of your being, every atom and every molecule. Make room for gratitude wherever you may reside. Be thankful. Appreciate the breaths you are gifted. This is the life that you live. You are only a temporary resident on a temporary residence. Take the hands off the clock and put them around those you value in your life and remember we are but a mere apparition in residency. Here today, gone tomorrow. Put your hands, heart, mind and soul around this life and its essence. "You can't give your life more time, so give the time you have left more life!"

Charlie Chaplin was quoted as saying, "We are all tourists, G-d is our travel agent who has already identified our routes, bookings and destinations… trust him and enjoy life. Life is just a journey! Therefore, live today! Tomorrow may not be."

Please be grateful and "Love what you have; before life teaches you to love what you lost." Sometimes you may not know the value of a moment until it becomes a memory. As Dr. Seuss shared, "to the world, you may be one person; but to one person, you may be the world."

Hashem gave you a fingerprint no one else has, so you can leave an imprint no one else can.

Inhale. Exhale. Let this be your first life-bursting breath after awakening from the spiritual comatose.

Here, take this: Gratitude XR is a new prescription in its extended release (XR) formula. Use daily for best results.

8

Soulcial Distancing

"In order to find the G-d that made man, we have to stop following the "gods" that man made."

If a tiny, microscopic virus like Covid-19 could cause such discomfort and damage, imagine what a little bit of emunah (faith) could do to comfort & repair!

People keep hiding and not seeking.

Hashem's work is everywhere. Just look around, "in my flesh I see Hashem" (Job 19:26).

While the world is in social distancing mode this is a time to not be distancing ourselves spiritually. We should be coming closer to Hashem. Keeping your distance from Hashem only promotes the spread of a spiritual respiratory virus called the yetzer hara (negative inclination).

All the masks, hand sanitizers and sheltering in place can't protect one from the real negativity that pervades and attacks the immune system. When sanitizing externally we should also consider sanitizing our hearts internally to rid ourselves of the virus of harsh judgments and hate.

So, if you can't go out, go within. If you must stay home then build from within.

Rabbi Freeman relates, "A home," wrote Solomon the Wise, "is built with wisdom." And not with a hammer. Because wisdom is the glue of beauty. Wisdom, meaning the ability to step back and see all of the picture, the past and, most important, the future to which all this leads. To see the truth inside each thing. Without wisdom, there are only fragments. With wisdom, there is a whole. And there is peace between all the parts of that whole.

Working on inner alignment neutralizes and diminishes the negativity, allowing positivity and peace to prevail. As quoted by the Vilna Gaon, the entire purpose of our existence is to overcome our negative habits. This includes the ongoing improvement of self-care related to physical, mental and spiritual hygiene. The aforementioned in conjunction with faith is a viricidal disinfectant.

Come closer. The greatest distance between people is misunderstanding. If we are sharing the same timeline of life on this earth now we should strive to be positive and forge a closer relationship with G-d and others. For, "The man who gives little with a smile gives more than the man who gives much with a frown."

As conveyed by Rashi, "Be soft. Do not let the world make you harsh. Do not let the pain make you hate. Do not let the bitterness steal your sweetness. Take pride that even though the rest of the world may disagree you still believe it to be a beautiful place." Life isn't about getting and having, it's about giving and being.

C. Jung said, "Thinking is difficult, that's why most people judge." Think about it. Put a hold on judging others and work on yourself. Cease following the "gods" that man made. Don't follow the crowd. They are lost.

Shavuos is a time of union and unification. A time to receive to give. Have heart and faith. Let's not fall prey to the sole separatists. As we stand together to receive the tree of life and light, the Torah, let our souls come closer to one another and Hashem.

9

Master Peace to Masterpiece

The Mishnah tells us, "Hashem did not find a more fitting vessel to contain blessing than shalom (peace)."

While there can be an elusiveness to peace, nonetheless, earnest exploration reveals peace can be found deep within & during the most trying of times. It's been mystically expressed, "Seek treasures amid ruins, sincere one. Seek wisdom that will untie your knot. Seek the path that demands your whole being."

Mirror or mirage? "What comes out when life squeezes you? When someone hurts or offends you? If anger, pain and fear come out of you, it's because that's what's inside. If you're irritated by every rub, how will your mirror be polished?" True peace is not rendered in times of stillness and when nothing is in conflict. On the contrary, real peace is being able remain still and relatively calm when all around you is in flux and not going the way you see fit. There's more power and peace in personal accountability than any amount of blame.

Make room for peace and let's please take time for some reflective introspection. Understand, nobody wants be lied to. But everyone has lied. Nobody wants to be stereotyped or judged. But everyone has stereotyped and judged. Nobody wants to be talked to or treated rudely. But everybody has talked to or treated somebody rudely. The things we demand from others should be equally applicable to ourselves. If you want better. Be better yourself. Do better. Highly hypocritical demanding from others what you don't even demand from yourself. Reflect. Find peace in congruency.

Yishuv hadaas (settled mind/tranquility) and menuchas hanefesh (serenity of the soul) are essential. There's no greater wealth in this world than peace of mind. Positive, peaceful thinking is free. Do more of it. As such one is able to process that until you change your thinking you're likely to recycle your experiences. A mind that is at peace is centered and not focused on harming others is stronger than any physical force. Yet many give credence and permission to outside physical forces to negatively galvanize them to act with reckless abandon, or any sense of care or respect towards self & others. These caustic reactions spur physical, mental and spiritual ruptures.

When reason is abdicated and replaced by caviling it hinders peaceful prospects.

It takes such temerity to deny the glaring truth in face of the current demonstrative, discordant evidence. The bloviating in all directions is clear. Don't allow the outside world to ravage your inner world. You can't put a price on peace of mind. Your life becomes a masterpiece when you learn to master peace. Let's learn to be more compassionate with each breath, there's only so much of it left. Also note, "a wise man once said nothing." One who is great is not ashamed to admit he does not know, said Rabbi Yehudah HaNasi.

Giving brings peace too. As the Chasidic proverb teaches, "Generosity does not make a person poorer." Also remember this proverb, If you have to choose between being kind and being right, choose being kind and you will always be right. It's also been pointed out that, "Apologizing does not always mean that you're wrong and the other person is right. It just means that you value your relationship more than your ego."

Rabbi Spira states that even when one is worthy of a bounty of blessings, if he engages in machlokes (conflict/arguments) the vessel is unable to contain the blessings. The receptacle is effectively riddled with holes; no matter how many wonderful things are poured into it, the vessel will remain empty because everything leaks right out.

Look. Listen. Learn. "Contentness is the new rich. Inner peace is the new success. Health is the new wealth. Kindness is the new cool."

I can be peace. You can be peace. We can be peace. Don't hurry. Don't worry. Do your best and let it rest.

Thus, seek peace and learn to carry life's difficulties with aplomb. Don't look to be acrimonious, argumentative and negative. A quiet act of restraint to avoid negativity and conflict speaks the loudest. Working to curtail irascibility demonstrates tranquility and ataraxy. Stop screaming and find meaning.

It's been expressed, "G-d writes spiritual mysteries on our hearts, where they wait silently for discovery." Actualize peace in this world of seeming contradictions. Strive to be symbiotic rather than parasitic. It's an inside job. Inherit the truth. Pray for peace and to become a proper vessel for blessing; for it's a work of the highest order. We must dovetail one into the other (blessing into peace). Keep working to master peace to make life a masterpiece.

10

Mystical Gems and Celestial Jewelry

The Arizal discusses the deeper reasons behind the mitzvos, tefillos (prayers) and kavanos (intentions/meditations) is to rectify the upper worlds, elevate the sparks and to unite/ interlace the Name(s) of HaKadosh Baruch Hu with the Shechina/Divine Presence and bring new light, energy, and fresh shefa (Divine flow/spiritual sustenance) to all creation.

Jewish mystical literature speaks about restoring the Shechina, which has been driven into exile because of our negative thoughts, speech and actions. In another sense, we are endeavoring to repair Adam's single sin/disconnect which had universal ramifications, as well as elevate the fallen nitzotzos, sparks. These sparks are fragments of divine vitality that are far from their original place that resulted from the shattering of the vessels. Our job is to raise the sparks, and build the Sefiros/Partzufim and worlds back up.

It's been broadcasted, "G-d first created the mystical Sefiros – 10 divine channels through which His infinite light could be condensed, contracted, and then released as individualized attributes that could eventually give rise to a diversity of finite creations. Also, the structure of the ten Sefiros exists in every world and in every person. In our quest to be in the Divine image we strive to model ourselves after the Sefiros (characteristics)."

Rabbi Fraenkel on the Nefesh HaChaim divulges that a one constantly creates (or destroys) many worlds with his thoughts, speech and actions having Supernal consequence.

Rabbi Afililo shares, the holy Ari relates that when a person does Mitzvos it causes two upper zivugim (unions). The first zivug is Abba & Imah and the second zivug is Zeir Anpin (Z'A) with Nukvah. The zivug of Abba/Chochma and Imah/Binah is accomplished through keeping the negative mitzvos/commandments. The zivug of Z'A (Chesed, Gevurah, Tiferes, Netzach, Hod, Yesod) and Nukvah (Malchus) is accomplished through performance of the positive mitzvos/commandments. Again, we are restoring and making connections, lights & vessels.

Rabbi Yitzchak Luria (the Ari) said the tikkunim (rectifications) in this world are for the purpose of causing Zeir Anpin and Nukvah to bond. For all we receive is manifest from the coupling of the them.

Hashem channels the needs of the physical world via the spiritual world(s).

The Torah reveals that the primary Name of G-d (HaShem) is the YHVH/Tetragramaton. According to our sources this Name encompasses everything. The

Tetragramaton is spelled by the four letters: Yud – Heh – Vav – Heh. The latter three letters (Heh-Vav-Heh) spell Hovei, which means "present" in Hebrew. While the first letter prefix "Yud" indicates future tense. Thus, the meaning of the Tetragramaton is that G-d is ever-present, i.e. eternal, He was, is, and always will be. It also connotes that G-d is constantly creating the present. HaShem is the underlying Source of all existence in the universe, points out Rabbi Yosef Sebag.

We must invariably do our utmost to connect and keep the YHVH in the equation.

Rabbi Shepherd discloses, Kabbalisticly there are four primary spiritual worlds and one even higher above them. The four primary spiritual worlds are Asiyah, Yetzirah, Beriah, and Atzilus. Above the aforementioned worlds, is the world of Adam Kadmon. How do they correspond to YHVH/Tetragrammaton and other mystical aspects? In descending order: The world of Adam Kadmon corresponds to the tip of the Yud [י], as well as the soul level of Yechida, the Sefirah of Keser (Crown), the Partzuf of Arich Anpin, and the Amidah. The world of Atzilus corresponds to the rest of the letter Yud [י], the soul level of Chaya, which relates to the Sefirah of Chochmah (Wisdom), the Partzuf of Abba, the Amidah plus the Shema and it's blessings, the mitzvah of head tefillin and the miluy (expansive spelling of YHVH) Av (72). The second letter of the Tetragrammaton Hey [ה] relates to the world of Beriyah, the soul level of Neshama, the Sefirah of Binah (Understanding), the Partzuf of Imma, the

Shema and it's blessings, the mitzvah of arm tefillin, the miluy of Sag (63). The third letter of the Tetragrammaton Vav [ו] corresponds to the world of Yetzirah, the soul level of Ruach, relates to the six lower Sefiros of Chesed, Gevurah, Tiferes, Netzach, Hod, Yesod, the Partzuf of Zeir Anpin, the verses of song, the mitzvah of Tallis, and the miluy of Mah (45). The fourth and last letter of the Tetragrammaton Hay [ה] relates to the world of Asiyah, the soul level of Nefesh, the Sefirah of Malchus (Kingdom), the Partzuf of Nukvah, the morning blessings/offerings, the mitzvah of relieving & washing and the miluy of Ban (52).

Rabbi Palvanov explains, according to Rabbi Yosef Karo that during our prayers, we ascend through the meta-physical universes until we stand before G-d, basking in Atzilus. Upon completion of the Amidah, we take three steps back to "descend" three levels back; each step in sequence from the worlds of Beriyah, Yetzirah, to our physical realm of Asiyah. This is equally applicable to the prayer service as the zenith is reached at the Amidah (Atzilus) and now new shefa levels back down (Beriyah, Yetzirah and Asiyah) from Ashrei (Beriyah), Shir shel yom (Yetzirah), Aleinu (Asiyah) until the end of the morning prayer service.

Furthermore, an added dimension in tefillah/prayer is that YHVH corresponds to partzuf Zeir Anpin/Z'A and ADNY corresponds to the partzuf Nukvah. Rabbi Rome teaches according to the Arizal, we think Hashem – YHVH, but verbalize the name as ADNY throughout tefillah, kavanos (mindful prayer) and meditation. This is an integrative process of the YHVH = light/ohr/Z'A and the ADNY = vessel/kli/Nukvah. Rabbi Chaim Vital explains, The Name YHVH (Hebrew: yud-heh-vav-heh) is associated with the six sefiros of Chesed/Kindness through Yesod/Foundation and represents the masculine principle, while the Name ADNY (Hebrew: alef-dalet-nun-yud) is associated with Malchus/Kingship and represents the feminine principle. Their unification brings harmony to each applicable "world " and the total structure of the sefiros on that plane by mentally combining the Divine Names YHVH and ADNY. The Ari teaches we meditate on the Name YHVH with its corresponding nekudos/vowels which also relates to a particular Sefirah. The Ari says this is a fundamental yichud (unification) is to bring the light of YHVH into the vessel(s) ADNY by the thought (*YHVH*/masculaine aspect) and verbalization (ADNY/feminine aspect). Plus, interwining the of the Names *YHVH* & ADNY – *YAHDVNHY* by interlacing (light & vessel) the two Divine Names and intergrating them together as one yichud. Another yichud says the Ari is that we should have the kavnnah of the final Hey of YHVH housing the letters/divine name ADNY.

The final bracha in the Amidah is shalom. Shalom is the vessel that holds all the other blessings. Rabbi Shepherd points out from the Ari that the letters of b'shalom can be rearranged to spell malbush which means garment indicating that we should mediate on enclothing the unity of all the blessings to protect it from the external forces.

The Ari also tells us when we say "Baruch Hoo, U'Baruch

Shemo" this is also a unification. Baruch is related to Yud. Hoo is related to Heh. U'Baruch is related to Vav and Shemo is related to Hey. Therefore when we say it all together a unification of the Yud to the Heh via "Baruch Hoo" and the Vav to the Hey via "U'Baruch Shemo" is made.

Another yichud/unification mentioned by the mystics is a meditation which focuses on the sanctity of every breath by thinking about the Name/Hashem/YHVH in the breathing cycle. Inhale: Yud/Hey. Exhale: Vav/Hey.

Using the Arizal's Kavannos for the 13 Attributes of Mercy – Rabbi Shepherd goes on, "we want to meditate to bring down the Divine flow from the upper world and reveal it in the lower world(s). The first time we say the name of Hashem is representative of the upper spiritual world. The second time we say the name of Hashem is representative of the lower spiritual worlds. Each of the 13 attributes we should think to bring down the flow from above to below. The Mekubalim teach us the highest inner and outward expression is to give pleasure to the Creator through the channels of machshava (thoughts), debore (speech) and miseay (actions). When we call upon Hashem via the 13 Attributes, we open the gates of compassion and are forgiven for any action of ours that is negative; also any harsh judgements are sweetened."

Other mystical gems shared by Rabbi Fraenkel are excavated from the Nefesh HaChaim and Rav Chaim's students, which discusses the meaning of the praise, "Amein. Yehay Shemey Rabba Mevorach…," which is an additional bestowal of blessings and supernal light on the four worlds of

Atzilus, Beriyah, Yetzirah and Asiyah. The sacred cascading continues when we say "LeOlam" as it relates to the world of Atzilus (Root of the Neshama) which then extends additional blessings to the level of "VeOlmay" which relates to the world of Beriyah and Yetzirah (also the soul levels of Neshama and Ruach). "Olmaya" relates to the world of Asiyah (soul level of Nefesh). Rav Chaim Volozhin continues, when one fully focuses his thoughts on this process it arouses additional holiness and blessings that impact all the aforementioned levels resulting in the eradication of sin from each of the three lower levels to the extent that it's as if they were never committed!

All the above mentioned is initiated and accomplished by having proper kavannah/intentions and positive, holy thoughts, speech and actions. Ultimately by polishing our middos/character traits via the Torah, the process of restoring the Shechina and repairing the world(s) is spiritually fabricated. As written in the Zohar, "The human voice is intimately tied to the Divine. The voice can summon forth both dark and Light forces. Different words and blessings resonate with the numerous supernal worlds that dwell on high, each realm bringing forth a particular ray of Divine Light to illuminate our existence. The entire lower world was created in the likeness of the higher world. All that exists in the higher world appears like an image in this lower world; yet all this is but One."

As above, so below. As below, so above. Reflectivity and

reciprocity. The prayer ascends and the blessing descends. The blessing ascends the abudance descends.

It's been revealed, "Meditate not to escape life, but so life does not escape us."

Rabbi Mimran shares, "The Gemora in Shabbos states that this world was created imperfect in order to give man the great honour of becoming a partner with HaShem Yisborach. Our limud haTorah, mitzvos, and ma'asim tovim, all achieve this very goal of rectifying this imperfect world. Included in this list is Tefilla. Our great Kabbalists have divulged to us that we do not simply pray three times a day but we pronounce a potent Tefilla by which one influences various spiritual spheres in order to accomplish this rectification and by doing so becomes a partner with HaShem Yisborach in the creation of this world."

These esoteric, cosmic treasures have been unearthed, gathered and refined by our holy Sages. The above mentioned are but a peak of what sparkles in the celestial treasure chest. The spirit-rituals will make your spirit "rich"-you-all! These priceless, glistening, spiritual gems bring the unified redemption ever closer.

Access this repository of spirituality and mystical ornamentations. Let's add life and dimension to our remaining years. Let's enliven and adorn the days and nights by striving to bring fresh consciousness, new light, unification and more shefa (spiritual sustenance). Take it in and give it out. Never cease seeking. Look it up, learn it up, and apply it in order to level up.

Pierce the cosmos. Drape the heavens. Become a spiritual *jew*eler. Shine.

11

Night Light

Before I leave the "house" (this world) I intend to keep a light on for others.

Why are you so surprised to find negativity and corruption running amok everywhere you look? This world is the coarsest and harshest of all worlds, the ultimate concealment of the Infinite Light. Almost all of it is darkness and emptiness. Only a tiny spark of good is buried deep within to sustain it. You could spend your lifetime dwelling on the outrages and scandals, the travesties and the rip-offs . . . — or you could take a moment to search for that spark. You could find it, grasp it, fan its flame. From within its aura, you will see the darkness shining brighter than the heavens. In that moment of light, the night will never have been, shared Rabbi Freeman. By penetrating the klipos, the shells, to reveal the innate light wrapped in the husks of the night we bring a new light that's indicative of the dawn.

Rav Kook sheds light by revealing, "Every man must know

and realize that inside of him burns a candle, and his candle is not the same as his friend's candle, and there is no one who does not have a candle. And every man must know and realize that he needs to strive to reveal the candlelight openly, and to kindle it into a great torch and light up the entire world."

My saintly father-in-law of blessed memory, HaRav Gavriel Finkel, zt"l, taught that each of us are like a candle. He shared, when one candle lights another candle, the first candles light is not diminished by lighting the other. In fact, it only serves to bring more light. To increase the illumination. We are each like a candle and should be willing to share our lights with one another. That way we can bring more light to the world. As it's been said, the darkness of the world cannot swallow the light of a glowing candle.

To dissolve the gloom we need to bring more light and less judgement.

We've become more judgmental and less compassionate in some ways. Maybe we should apply to ourselves that which we demand of others. We can't change anyone, the least we could do is not judge them.

Rabbi Silverstein related, "If we spent less time trying to make this world a better place to live in, and more time trying to make ourselves better people to live with, the world would be a better place to live in." Be kind to yourself and include others too. Sling kindness around like confetti. Decorate yourself and the world with it!

Kabbalah teaches that when bad things happen to good

people and or innocent children, we must remember that we are in a partnership with the Infinite. Our response must be to focus the Light within us toward the uplifting of the fallen, the broken, the wounded and the shattered, from the darkness of the sitra achra, through the mitzvos of Gemilus Chasadim (deeds of lovingkindness) and the sharing of Chochmas HaLev (Wisdom of the Heart). Together we strive for a deeper unity. We are not alone in this work.

An insightful rabbi said, "The measure of human character is our reaction to dark times. No one can sidestep darkness. It is the throne upon which light sits. If a soul has not known sadness and struggle, there is no chance of overcoming, no cherishing the dawn."

The dark is punctuated by the light. The light is punctuated by the dark.

There is no amount of darkness that can outshine the light.

Become a "light"house. If we all learned to leave our "lights" on before we left the "house" the world would be a much more de*light*ful and illuminated place. The judgments would be tempered with each of our unified lights to see the way home through the darkest of nights.

12

I Thank Therefore I Am

"I thank therefore I am" proclaims Rabbi Siegel. This spin on Descartes' "I think therefore I am" is apropos at this timeframe from my perspective.

I often "think" what a gift it is to be alive right now with all that's going on. It need not be delineated. We all see it, hear it and feel it. All of us together sharing the same timeline of unfolding events on this planet.

What say you?! Have your senses not yet been bled dry or satiated? Are your eyes and ears flooded on overload? Be not saddened or disheartened. These times are but the birth pangs of greater things to come. Change makes noise; not the change in pocket, but the change within. Are you living with the delusion that you and things are meant to be perfect? Additionally, "Apologizing does not always mean that you're wrong and the other person is right. It just means that you value your relationship more than your ego." You don't have to always be all right to be alright. Connectivity and compassion sweeten the strict judgements.

Rabbi Freeman shares, if you were meant to be perfect, your soul would have remained in its heavenly womb. But no, here you are on earth, a divine soul that has infiltrated across the boundary of worlds, compressed itself into a body of meat and blood, wrestling each day with the biochemistry of an upright animal, struggling to bring some light into a cold and dark world, to squeeze even a single moment of pure goodness out of the beast – for even one altruistic moment in an entire lifetime makes it all worthwhile. From your every small victory, the world is transformed.

Also, be thankful for closed doors & detours. They protect you from paths and places that were not meant for you.

Pause and contemplate the simple words, "thank you." These words are a prayer, blessing, appreciation, sanctification, and expression. People from all over the world utter them in various life circumstances, finding meaning, strength, and direct access to Hashem.

Be thankful for what you have. Be thankful for what you don't have. Give thanks you can give thanks. Just try living being thankful.

Thank you for reading this.

13

Anatomical Miracle:Symphony No.1 in 613 Movements

The human body is a miraculous apparatus of synchronization. The mere engineering and harmony of the parts and its whole are a marvel; each individual part playing its symphonic instrumentation making a melodious contribution to the function of the human body as a complete work of art. A biological musical score of opus and corpus. Amazing, breathtaking, and utterly captivating is this human body in which each of us is implanted. The intricacies woven into the fabric of the human body are a brilliant design which points to a Prime Mover, One Conductor of such a divine symphony of anatomy and physiology; a skeletal/ muscular cantata, called the human body/life.

Consider the concerto, some of its crescendos and the design of this grand oeuvre: "The average red blood cell lives for 120 days. There are 2.5 trillion (give or take) of red blood cells in your body at any moment. To maintain this number, about two and a half million new ones need to be produced every second by your bone marrow. Considering all the tissues and cells in your body, 25 million new cells are being produced each second. A red blood cell can circumnavigate your body in less than 45 seconds. Nerve impulses travel at over 400 km/hr (25 miles/hr). A sneeze generates a wind of 166 km/hr (100 miles/hr), and a cough moves out at 100 km/hr (60 miles/hr). Our heart beats around 100,000 times every day .Our blood is on a 60,000-mile journey. Our eyes can distinguish up to one million color surfaces and take in more information than the largest telescope known to man. Our lungs inhale over two million liters of air every day, without even thinking. We give birth to 100 billion red cells every day. When we touch something, we send a message to our brain at 124 mph. We exercise at least 30 muscles when we smile. We are about 70 percent water. We make one liter of saliva a day. Our nose is our personal air-conditioning system: it warms cold air, cools hot air and filters impurities. In one square inch of our hand we have nine feet of blood vessels, 600 pain sensors, 9000 nerve endings, 36 heat sensors and 75 pressure sensors. One square inch of human skin contains 625 sweat glands. The aorta, the largest artery in the body, is almost the diameter of a garden hose. Capillaries, on the other hand, are so small that it takes ten of them to equal the thickness of a human hair. Your body has about 5.6 liters (6 quarts) of blood. 5.6 liters of blood circulates through the body three times every minute.

The heart pumps about 1 million barrels of blood during an average lifetime – that's enough to fill more than 3 super tankers. Babies start dreaming even before they're born. 10% of human dry weight comes from bacteria. In 24 hours, the blood in the body travels a total of 12,000 miles – that's four times the width of North America. The DNA helix measures 80 billionths of an inch wide. You breathe in about 7 quarts of air every minute. In 30 minutes, the average body gives off enough heat (combined) to bring a half gallon of water to boil." This is all composed and conducted without the Maestro sweating one iota!

Above are but a few collected notes in the divinely inspired composition. Such a sonata and splendid arrangement deserves the attention of all our senses. The string (limbs) and wind instruments (air and breathing capacity) take center stage in this concert hall called "life." The human body has been broadcasted to enclose 613 limbs and sinews (248 limbs/ positive commandments and 365 sinews/negative commandments). 613 movements- 613 Mitzvos.

Rabbi Chaim Vital spotlights in Shaarei Kedusha: "The same way a tailor crafts a physical garment related to the contours of the body, Hashem similarly constructed the body, which is the garment of the soul, in the shape of the soul; with 248 limbs and 365 tendons corresponding to 248 spiritual limbs & 365 spiritual tendons. When performing a particular mitzvah (physically) it nourishes that particular spiritual limb/ tendon on a metaphysical level."

Misuse of this symphony called the anatomical miracle is

hard to hear. The discordance between the body and soul can be cacophonous.

Immoral self indulgence of the body as noted at the close of last week's & in the opening of this week's parsha (Pinchas) ultimately imparted a grave elegy. However, as difficult as it may be to hear, the alacritous decision by Pinchas seemingly re-synchronized the symphony of body (and soul), as he was rewarded the priesthood as a result.

King David transcribed, "You made all the delicate, inner parts of my body and knit me together in my mother's womb. Thank You for making me so wonderfully complex! Your workmanship is marvelous — how well I know it. You watched me as I was being formed in utter seclusion, as I was woven together in the dark of the womb. You saw me before I was born. Every day of my life was recorded in Your book. Every moment was laid out before a single day had passed" [Psalms 139:13-16].

The sheet music is the Torah. The body (and soul) is one symphony in 613 movements; a gross anatomical ensemble. The opportunity to align such a composition as the human body with its Creator permits this magnum opus to be experienced in its full fruition, the body harmoniously at work in concert with the soul. The anatomy of a miracle is discovered in the miracle of the anatomy. A body fill-harmonic. An orchestration of the Most High. A Masterpiece of Infinite proportion!

14

Me-No-Rah

Ahh Chanukah! The miracles. The oil. The Menorah. The sensations of sweet victory. Two thousand plus years of beautiful, meaningful history & heritage ignited. A trail, a clear path of well lit candles lighting the way; passed on from generation to generation.

A central piece at Chanukah is the menorah. The miracle itself lasted eight days – and to commemorate this, we light on Chanukah an eight-branched Menorah. The traditional Chanukah menorah is unique in it's U shape structure. There are 8 branches which form 4 U's in the U shaped Chanukah menorah.

Linking the four U shaped arms of the menorah to the four Worlds of Kabbalah we ignite something as fascinating as it is esoterically penetrating.

The four Worlds are Atzilus, Beriah, Yetzirah & Asiyah. Atzilus (Emanation) – the eternal unchanging Divine world. Beriah (Creation) – it is the first separation from the Divine and the world of souls. Yetzirah (Formation) – the abode of the angels. Asiyah (Action) – the material universe in which we live and its earthly substance.

Spiritual electricity sheds holy sparks and is in constant flow from each of the four Worlds and the Sefiros, from its most spiritual, to its most material. Unified and perpetually candescent.

G-d's infinite light kindles all existence and dispels darkness.

Chanukah represents the transition from darkness to light. The four Worlds are vivified as we light the menorah; dispelling the dark both spiritually and physically. Each night a light in the physical and spiritual world(s) is touched off. The shamesh. which is the central stem, can be emblematic of the Ohr (Light) of the Ein Sof (Infinity) as it stands at the center (nucleus) of the menorah and all the world(s), partzufim, sefiros, etc. Furthermore, the shamesh gives light to the unlit candles and hence illuminates the aforementioned. A glowing impression shines forth as we emanate, create, form and act in the unison with Infinity to fuel and burnish a path towards goodness.

P. Namanworth throws light on the matter at hand, "We are all flames on the Menorah. Chanukah focuses our meditations and practice on realizing the flame within us, the mission that is uniquely ours-to spread light wherever we go. We don't want to just light the Menorah, we want to be a Menorah. To be aware of our G-dly soul and purpose and to share that light wherever we go. He continues, to be a lamp-lighter we need to have access to the deep pool of oil within us, the deep resources of holiness and sanctity that are not limited by nature, but in fact, are unlimited. By accessing this deep reservoir of infinity we maintain a steady connection to our deep unconscious, the place where opposites reside together. Where the depth of our potential is revealed. The sense that we are more than we think we are and can achieve greater things each day because we were put on this earth to make a difference, to make a dwelling place for G-d in this lowest world. This is the story the flames tell us on Chanukah. You are truly free when you can access the deepest dimensions of your soul."

Each of the the candles represents one of the characteristics (Sefiros). Each of us has a personality that leans more toward one or more of these Sefiros/attributes than the others. This combination makes us uniquely who we are.

Rabbi Nefesh relates that from a Jewish mystical standpoint the lights revealed on Chanukah are as follows: First night of Chanukah – We receive the Light of Malchus in the Vessel of Binah. We light 2 candles (1 candle & Shamash/server candle) after nightfall. Second night – Receiving Light of Yesod in Vessel of Chesed We Light 3 candles (2 candles and Shamash). Third night – Receiving Light of Hod in Vessel of Gevurah. We Light 4 candles (3+1). Fourth night – Receiving Light of Netzach in Vessel of Tiferes. We Light 5 candles (4+1). Fifth night – Receiving Light of Tiferet in Vessel of Netzach. We Light 6 candles (5+1). Sixth night – Receiving Light of Gevurah in Vessel of

Hod. We Light 7 candles (6+1). Seventh night – Receiving Light of Chesed in the Vessel of Yesod. We Light 8 candles (7+1). Eighth night – Receiving Light of Binah in the Vessel of Malchus. We Light 9 candles (8+1).

He continues, "The most important connection is drawing Light to the Vessel. We use oil that represents the Light of Chochmah coming through Binah. The miracle that was revealed and re-appears every year during this time is a continuous flow of Light from Binah to Malchus."

Chanukah in this light becomes a beautiful mystical marriage of spirit and matter. G–d (Infinite) and humankind (finite).

To move from me-know-rah (darkness) to me-no-rah (light) is a message burning deep within Chanukah and the Menorah, and is an expression of inextinguishable, unquenchable luminosity.

A radiant distinction is now illuminated. One can decipher between positive and negative, tov (good) and rah (evil) through the medium of the Menorah. We therefore extinguish the "rah" by lighting the Menorah- Me-No-Rah.

Don't let your hopes be dimmed.

Chanukah and the menorah shed a brilliant, clinquant light upon the tenebrosity. The darkness dissipates under the lights and we are given a blazing trail towards goodness, and as result distance ourselves from negativity. Me-no-rah (evil). Hear no rah. See no rah. Speak no rah. This is the dazzling, effulgence of the Chanukah menorah. Eight days/night can be emblematic of the 8 lights which "ate"/consumed the night; a recipe for hope and continuity. Eight is a number that transcends the natural/finite. Eight represents that which is beyond nature. All finite existence comes to life via the infinite Light.

Rabbi Pinson ignites with a beautiful insight, "The Hebrew word Nefesh/Soul, is comprised of three Hebrew letters: Nun, Pei, and Shin. These letters are an acronym for: Ner/Flame. Pesilah/Wick. Shemen/Oil. The Flame is our Soul. The Oil is our Passion. The Wick is Action. Just a as a flame cannot manifest without a wick and oil, in order to manifest our soul, our spirit, we must attach it to a Wick, a physical action, and we need the Oil, the passion to unify the Spirit (Flame) with the physicality (Wick)."

Chanukah is a time of year to get fired up. It's gonna be "lit!"

May we unify the light of our soul with our body and our world. Ignite the night. Set the world aglow with a G-dly light.

15

Spiritual "Contact" Lenses (More Than Meets the Eye)

The Torah, the Prophets, the Writings, the Mishnah, the Gemara, Aggadah, the Midrash and numerous other Judaic sources are replete with stories and laws. Each and every story and law in all the compendiums of Jewish thought, including the verbal transmissions with its various nuances, whether revealed or hidden, orbits around one common predication: there is a spiritual reality called G-d.

Every single story that imparts a lesson and/or Halacha (Jewish law) that tells us how to live, informs us in some capacity how draw closer to the infinite, Unified Essence of G-d as we understand it from our limited finite perspective (ie. from spiritual vessels/attributes called in Kabbalistic literature the Sefiros).

It states in Bereshis 1:26, man was created in "G-d's image."

Hashem has no image whatsoever. So, what does this mean practically?

Jewish mystical sources elucidate we are formed as a reflection of the G-d's characteristics &/or attributes. This finite formula is manifested/revealed through the Sefiros, their combinations/interrelationships. The Sefiros are Keser (Crown), Chochmah (Wisdom), Binah (Understanding), Daas (Knowledge), Chesed (Kindness), Gevurah (Strength), Tiferes (Beauty), Hod (Splendor), Netzach (Victory), Yesod (Foundation) & Malchus (Kingship). Each of these represent one aspect (so to speak) of the Ain Sof's Divine attributes with which the world(s) are governed through judgement, kindness and/or mercy. Each sefirah is also identified with a part of the body or facet of the human personality, a color, and one of the Names of the Holy One.

The aforementioned & so much more is talked about in great length, breadth & depth in the Arizal's (Rabbi Yitzchak Luria) writings (most of which extends far beyond my understanding). Nevertheless, the Ari & many other Kabbalists enlighten us that part of being created in "G-d's image" means we have the power(s) to exercise our free-will to "emulate" G-d by aligning and balancing the/our Sefiros by way & means of performing mitzvos, learning Torah, tefillah (prayer) and trying to improve our character traits. By doing so, this in turn can generate some positive influence in/ on the world(s) which consequently activates more blessing(s) from Hashem. Moreover, this aids us in our emulation and dveykus (cleaving) to Hashem.

Systemically, the sefiros can be drawn down from an ethereal, spiritual plane to a conceptual plane, from a conceptual plane to a psychological plane & finally into some tangibility in our lives on a behavioral (physical) plane. The sefiros as such are part of our intellectual, emotional, behavioral makeup/ attributes. Rabbi Feder relates, "G-d creates the world and reveals Himself by enclothing His Infinite Light in ten attributes that parallel human characteristics." These attributes are the Sefiros. Through integration and application, the lessons of the Sefiros can act as template on a human level and with it we can begin the journey to self-improvement and a deeper, more meaningful relationship with Hashem.

Kabbalah is an aspect of Torah, and Torah means "guidance" or "instructions." Kabbalah provides a cosmic dimension to the issues of everyday human life. The challenges in life are the sparks lost in the primal act of creation, coming to you to be repaired and elevated. Your life is a mission, in which you are directed to the divine sparks that belong uniquely to your soul, for which your soul has returned many times to this world until they will all be gathered. Understanding the cosmic dimension means that nothing in life is trivial. Everything has meaning. Everything moves toward a single purpose, with a single goal. Understanding allows you to take on those challenges and to complete the journey of your soul, said Rabbi Freeman.

We should endeavor to perceive the hidden through that which is revealed. From our perspective this is so we can overcome the Sitra Achra (negative side) through Mitzvah performance.

From a Jewish mystical perspective, it's been said that the intersection between opposites is described as process whose purpose is to bring about a greater wholeness and unity. The purpose of the breaking is repair; the purpose of Tzimtzum, or contraction, is to make room and lead to renewed expansion; the purpose of darkness is to uncover light. Human beings have a role in revealing the hidden good and actualizing it. We are called to recognize the divine source of our souls and provide a link between heaven and earth.

Dr. C. Jung shared, "Your visions will become clear when you can look inward into your own heart. Who looks outside, dreams; who looks inside; awakes."

Got spirituality? Get spiritualized!

It's such a blessing to be connected to the Source. Our heritage is so multifaceted. So many dimensions & levels! It's difficult to encapsulate with words the profound mystical beauty that is woven into our roots. Learning and growing through mitzvos, Torah study and prayer opens pathways to the esoteric conduits of light thereby deepening & enriching our symbiotic-like relationship with Hashem. There is more to being Jewish than meets the eye! It's transforming and transcendental. These are the real "contact"(with the Infinite) lenses. Seeing goes far beyond the field of vision. Mystically speaking, there's no end in sight.

16

Bringers of the Horizon

What is our role during this short existence?

We live as if we're guaranteed another breath, another second, another minute, another hour, another day, month and year. At times taking so many things for granted. Even now, the fact that you can see, read and comprehend this is a blessing. How easy we forget.

Moreover, we judge and hold grudges while being held captive by a host of negative attitudes. Anger, arguments and irritability becomes commonplace. Espousing slander and gossip exposes egocentricity and weakness. Flippancy and bitterness thrive. And then, we're gone. Having harbored darkness and negativity, we exit or loved one's depart. Having lived so physically preoccupied with "self" we're left alone with the bone chilling reality and guilt. And so, as the sun begins to set we've mastered the fine art of dwelling with a false sense of security in intelligence, politics, money, status, arts & entertainment, all of which is ultimately vain and nugatory if not kept in check.

Rebbe Nachman in Sichos Haran #51, "There is no need to be upset about whether or not you have money. Even with money, you could waste away your days. The world deceives us completely. It makes us think we are constantly gaining, but we end up with nothing. People spend years working to make money, but in the end, when they come to the final reckoning, they are left with nothing in their hands. Even when someone becomes "rich," in the end he is taken from his money. Man and money cannot remain together. Either the money is taken from the man or the man from his money. No- one has ever stayed with his money. Where is all the money people have been making since the beginning of time? People have always been busy making money – so where is all the money? It has all become absolutely nothing!" He also said, "Worldly riches are like nuts; many a tooth is broke in cracking them, but never is the stomach filled with eating them." And so, you're not truly "rich" until you have what money can't buy. Priceless advice, "It costs \$0.00 to be a decent human being."

There are two desires. Physical desire and Spiritual desire.

Those solely preoccupied with the physical are driven by the physical. What you drive, ends up driving you. What you own, ends up owning you. What you feel physically empowers, can actually weaken and distance oneself if not infused with a spiritual paradigm.

Not only do we need to earn a living, we also need to earn a life.

Spiritual proclivities and desires produce more room internally and externally. Broadening the horizon is about becoming more expansive, more spiritual. The less "self," the more health.

Hashem's purpose for creating the world was to give pleasure to its creatures, to know the Truth through cultivating a relationship with Hashem, and to receive all the pleasantness prepared for each of us accordingly. This is done by elevating and connecting the physical to the spiritual. As it's been said, "We are not human beings having a spiritual experience. We are spiritual beings having a human experience."

Life can be so much more than cognitive distortions, defense mechanisms and self absorption with continued work, sensitivity and awareness.

It's "Modeh Ani" in the beginning and "Yisgadal v'yiskadash" in the end. It's what we do in between that makes all the difference.

Rabbi Freeman insightfully shares, "Each of us is allocated from above just the amount of time we need to get our mission done. Some of that time will be for learning, teaching, helping others. Some of that time will be needed for making a living, which is also a divine task with purpose and meaning. But none of us can justify our obsession with making a living by claiming that it leaves no time to learn or to teach. This is nothing less than misappropriation of funds;

by spending all the allotted time on one task at the expense of your principal purpose in this world. Each of us is foremost a student and a teacher."

We have many roles to play prior to our death. Furthermore, none of us know when we're going to go. It's as if each of us have an abstract/invisible digital clock lingering above our heads counting down. Each of us scheduled for a different time of departure, unbeknownst to one another.

Let's fill the role of seeking and creating peace. Don't leave this earth or let loved ones slip away without minimizing the physical/negative attitudes and maximizing the spiritual. Try to make amends. Work on the relationship. Forgive yourself. Forgive others. Make room for Hashem and others. We receive to give. We give to receive. As stated in the Zohar, "Every action in this physical dimension has a corresponding influence in the Upper Worlds. In truth, both worlds are actually one reality; they are like reflections in a mirror. The Light is aroused and then reflected back to us in the physical world to refine and perfect our souls." Light begets light. Darkness begets darkness.

Make yourself into a vessel and prepare new vessels for the Light with positive thoughts, speech and actions.

As expressed in the Zohar, "The budding and blossoming of a flower reflects the process of creation that unfolds in the Upper World as well as the Lower World, which is our physical universe. As a seed contains the entire flower, the original thought of creation contains the creation as a whole, including its final and complete perfection."

What's on the horizon is activated by what we do on the horizontal, this plane of existence; how we treat others and our relationship with Hashem. In order to light up the horizon with the most brilliant colors & lights we must diminish our own animalistic, self centered desires. For in a person so full of himself there is no space for G-d or anything/anyone else. With all due respect, it's not all about you or me. It's about us & Hashem. The bringers of the horizon. By making earth a dwelling place for the Shechina (Divine Presence) we become a light unto the nations on all horizons.

Unify duality.

Endeavoring to make the physical subservient to the spiritual is to bring a new dawn and an illuminative glow to this existence by making positive use of the short time we have here on earth & to bring the horizon home, back to its Source. By striving to connect the horizontal to vertical we stand in unity on the horizon of a new day rising.

17

Dig Deep

"The strength of my soul was born on the backs of moments that brought me to my knees."

The longer we live the more we will experience the death of others. This is a fact of life (& death). A bittersweet blessing in that we're still here, but sad that the dearly departed are not. We should inculcate the lessons of standing at the graveside of our loved ones as they make their gradual physical descent into the designated plot. Let's remember the thoughts and feelings that penetrated our core and try to live accordingly. Let's use the profound lessons of death, for enhancing life.

Sometimes we must dig deep to unearth the sweet.

Rav Kook schools us on death from a novel perspective. Death is a false phenomenon. What makes death unclean is that it spreads an aura of falsehood. Actually, what people call death is the opposite: an ascent into an even greater and more real life. We are plunged into the depths of small-mindedness.

What has placed us here? Our physical and emotional drives. These drives, gazing upon this ascent into life, interpret it as a dreadful, black phenomenon that they label: death.

Rabbi Freeman speaks with such inspirational strength, "You are not here to find love, nor to be greeted by happiness at every turn, nor to be showered with kindness, nor to be celebrated by all, to forever remain a child. No. You came here to create love out of war. Your soul willingly left its blissful place beyond all troubles to descend into a stifling frame of bone, blood and flesh. Why? Because only here can inner strength be forged by pain, can wisdom be nurtured by failure, can love be the reward of those who choose to give love. Your soul came here to struggle with the bitter things of life and squeeze out of them a syrup of sweet, inner joy. And as there is no sweetness as succulent as bittersweet, so there is no river of love that runs as deep as the love forged through a battle of the heart, no strength as powerful as that wrestled from the hands of an enemy through stubborn, defiant resolve, no wisdom as the wisdom gained by stumbling in darkness, standing up again, stumbling and walking again, and again. All that is good, all that has meaning, all is up to you alone."

We mold the soul with thoughts, speech and actions. What seems like death can ultimately teach about & give life. Digging deep we find this is illustrated in the story of Passover.

Rabbi Tzion explains, the month Nissan gives us the holiday of Passover that is a celebration of freedom &

emancipation from the negative side. The coming back to light and life. It represents the complete revelation of the light of Chesed. We learn that on Nisan we can have a spiritual birth. Rabbi Chaim Vital, the student of the Ari, said that these days are like the birth of coming out of Egypt. We should be positive and act with Chesed/kindness. We 'plant' positive roots for the entire year and renew our lives. Strive to be pure and sincere with your consciousness and actions.

The ultimate liberation will come through the channels of compassion and not judgment.

Digging ever deeper we discoverer life beyond life. Life beyond the grave. We must try to take these redemptive lessons of Passover and physical death to enhance and modify life while we're alive in this world. Take heed the lessons of death and slavery. Learn to sculpt it into life (light) and true freedom. Then, the angel of death may pass-over us. Rabbi Rom relates, kabbalistically to bring Hashem's love, light and healing into this world, there needs to be a zivug/unification between Zeir Anpin and the Nukva. But Zeir Anpin cannot have a zivug without Mochin/Divine Consciousness. No mochin or restricted/immature mochin = trapped in Egypt. Indicating, increased judgment and narrow mindedness, brought about by negative, egocentric energy and selfish behavior. We should set out to bring shefa/abundance and expansive mind/mature mochin to Z"A which will flow to Nukvah/Malchus (and the world) by using kavannah (sincere intention) and the Mitzvos outlined in the Torah. Our souls strength is forged on struggles and strife that can sometimes make us feel as if we're being brought to our knees. Just when we think it's most darkest, the dawn peeks over the skyline signifying redemption and hope.

Passover is about living free. Those that have "passed-over" to the other side know the truth and are free from the physical snares & confines.

Look around the shore for seashells. Look around the world to see shells.

The choppy seas of our life can split revealing a clear path to healing and redemption. We must dig deep within ourselves, outside ourselves, beyond the grave & the physical. Toiling to break the slave chains in order to excavate & reveal a life far deeper and exponentially more meaningful. Take a moment to consider, "All the water in the in all the oceans can't sink a ship unless it gets inside the ship. Similarly, all the negativity of the world can't put you down unless you allow it to get inside you."

Let's remember we're all essential. Dig deeper than yourself and you might find what you're looking for.

During these trying times of peril and quarantine it's as if Hashem is saying, "Now that I've cleared your schedule, let's talk."

X marks the spot. All the treasures are here. One must only dig deeper.

If you've got time on your hands, put your hands on the time. It can be likened to using a pottery wheel with a block of unmolded clay. The clay representing (one's time/life). If one sets the wheel in motion without putting his/her hands on the clay (life & time) the wheel will rapidly spin and the clay will be chaotically strewn about the room making a mess. However, if one puts his/her hands on the clay (one's time) and molds & sculpts the clay (the time/life) then it can be fashioned into something beautiful and meaningful. Put your "hands" on your life this time. Participate in shaping a better, positive life/time for yourself and others.

Our strength is born and cultivated by delving into reservoirs of our souls; digging deep into the essence of our being. The tribulations are growing pains. We bend, but we're not broken.

May we use Pesach and all of our time productively to overcome the deathly, negative inclinations and see(k) the Light in everything.

~ *In memory of the dearly departed and may the ailing have a speedy & full recovery.*

18

Life³ [Cubed]

Life³ = Life x life x life = Life to the power of three = 'three' dimensions = Physical life, mental life, and spiritual life = Nefesh (actions), ruach (speech/emotions), and neshama (thoughts). Life can be cubed on numerous tiers and gradients.

Life often contains puzzling twist & turns. Flummoxed and discombobulated one is left not feeling right.

Can you spare some change? Thinking a way you've never thought before. Feeling a way you've never felt before. Seeing what you've never seen before. Hearing what you've never heard before. Becoming what you never were before. Being what you've never been before.

How each individual chooses and translates the aforementioned into their own of "cube" of existence determines various outcomes. The enigma of life unfolds in momentary increments of time. The mystery shifts and forms "my-story" (each individual's personal life story).

Finding solutions on the cube of life can be likened to solving the Rubik's Cube which is a 'three'-dimensional puzzle. Each cube consists of different sides/colors. They all interlock to form one big cube. The object of the game is to turn the cube(s) in such a way that each side has all the cube(s) of one particular color. In the larger "cube" or puzzle called life we are only apportioned a certain block/cube of time to live. Again, how we manage all the "colors" and "sides" (various life situations) will reveal congruency or incongruency.

Our mindset is important. Think of the algorithms as moving a piece out of the way, setting up its correct position, and then moving the piece into that place. Kabbalistically, Rabbi Wisnefsky indicates, the purpose of any intellectual insight and the resultant revamping of one's world-view is to remake the individual to the extent to which one has an emotional relationship (with the intellectual insight) and a positive response to reality that is being restructured. The development of new psychospiritual mentalities progresses through 'three' stages: embryonic mentality, nursing mentality and mature mentality. The progression from one stage to next is predicated on the displacement of the old mentality with a new mentality. Look for the patterns in life and adjust accordingly. Reconfigure. Try to take into consideration all angles and aspects.

An interesting set of twist and turns takes place as Moshe received his mission at the Burning Bush. At its conclusion, Moshe, fortified to the power of 'three' with three signs and

Hashem's assurance was prepared to confront Pharaoh. The three signs would materialize as miracles he could perform at will before the people to convince them that he indeed was the man to lead them out of Egypt. The first sign was a staff that Moshe would heave to the ground, where it would transform into a serpent. When he grasped the serpent by the tail, it reverted to a stick. The second was that when Moshe thrust his hand into his chest, it contracted leprosy. When he returned it to his chest, it reverted to its healthy state. Finally, Moshe was to take some of the waters of the Nile and decant it onto dry land, where it would convert to blood. The three signs could be approached from this angle: Firstly, a staff which is an inanimate object becomes a snake, which is an animate living creature. Secondly, the ability the take that which is disease ridden flesh and restore flesh to health. Thirdly, taking liquid, that being water, and transforming into the physical life-force called blood. Rotating and linking the three dimensions of our earthly existence with the three signs presents a solution-based outcome to the initial puzzling set of circumstances. In summation, the first sign is animation (and also could indicate dominion over the snake ie. yetzer hara/negative inclination). The second sign is of flesh. The third sign is blood. What can be gleaned from these 'three' signs? It could be put forward, that following the pathways prescribed in the Torah sets a mixed-up world in order, as it animates the flesh and blood on this three dimensional plane of existence by providing step by step directives to subdue the yetzer hara. Also, it's the instruction manual for decoding and connecting earthliness to spirituality. The instructions in the Torah are what truly animates and elevates the physical (flesh & blood) to live a more mindful, spiritual life on a nefesh, ruach and neshama level.

As previously mentioned, life encompasses a surfeit of twist and turns creating all sorts of patterns. At times when it appears, we have solved one of life's quandaries, another problem appears. And so, we continue to shift and turn life's "cube" in attempt to make the sides match up. In order to come to some solution we need to utilize the *soul*utions in the Torah, which in turn, will justly animate & guide life in the nefesh (flesh/blood/actions), ruach (speech/emotions) and neshama (intellect/thought). Using these solutions we are able to decipher life's puzzling twists and turns. Life does come with an instruction manual. The directions in the Torah adds meaning to the permutations, while orienting all sides of this 3d "cube"called life. From a maze to amazed, "turn" it all over to Hashem. Life[3] on this cube called life, *soul*ved.

19

MellowDramatic

How do we no longer get caught up in the drama of this world?

The Leshem, Rav Shlomo Elyashiv zatzl, indicates in that there are four stages by way of two emanations and two contractions. The aforesaid are the lights and vessels of existence. The sod of the four tiers are the secrecy of the name of Hashem YHVH, which G-d reveals in every revelation and is the soul/sole root of all the worlds. It's all Hashem.

In the words of the Zohar there is a higher unity. Meaning, that everything is One. At the root is Ain Sof/Infinity, there is only the Oneness of Hashem, the Infinite One.

Rav Pinson denotes that this is what is expressed in Shema Yisrael Hashem Elokeinu Hashem Echad. Only Hashem, Oneness. And the expression of Hashem's presence in this world is in the second line, Baruch Shem Kavod Malchuso Le'Olam Vaed, which indicates there is a world and existence which Hashem's light continues to permeates and vivify the entirety of existence. Rav Pinson indicates that Shema Yisrael… is, only Hashem exists. Baruch Shem… is, I exist because of Hashem. I exist because there is a Creator. So, Yesh there is, something, existence (Baruch Shem…) & from a deeper level of Ayin No-Thing only Hashem exists (Shema Yisrael…).

Rav Pinson continues, the first stage is we are completely connected to the drama and the life of this world. Constant movement and change. One day you're happy. The next you're sad, upset. This happens, that happens, we're constantly in different states. There are different colors, imagery, sound, tastes and states. We are all born this way. This is the expression of Baruch Shem Kavod Malchuso LeOlam Vaed. We live in this world of movement and try to connect to Hashem.

Then there's a higher state or level where everything is stillness, One. Life, death, this, that, it's all the same. That's, Shema Yisrael Hashem Elokeinu Hashem Echad. It's only Hashem.

Avraham was able to reach a level where he recognized everything was the absolute Oneness of Hashem. From the point of Ayin No-Thing, only Hashem (Shema Yisrael…) and then he chose to come back to (Baruch Shem…) and do chesed on a terrestrial level. He started from the world of movement. Entered the world of stillness and chose to return to the world of movement. This Rav Pinson conveys is remaining still, in Hashem's Oneness celestial (Shema

Yisrael…) and returning in movement to terrestrial (Baruch Shem…).

Hashem is One on every level of creation and in every world. The differentiations are only from our limited finite standpoint. The entire cosmos is with you. It evolves through the way you face and overcome the challenges of life. To be able to work on bridging and bringing the Oneness from stillness to movement as Avraham did is no easy task. To be able to sincerely espouse and bring from stillness, Shema Yisrael Hashem Elokeinu Hashem Echad. To movement, Baruch Shem Kavod Malchuso LeOlam Vaed is our life's work; to be able to take all the earthly drama and not let it get to us and ultimately recognize it's all from Hashem is a calling of the highest order. To move from melodramatic to mellow dramatic is to recognize and integrate it's only Hashem; always was, is & will be the One true King of all drama.

20

Shedding Skin

In biology, molting is the process by which species/animals cast off skin or a part of its body to unearth a newer version. This process is initiated during seasonal time frames or junctures in its life cycle.

Rosh Hashana is "the head of the year." The head anatomically is placed above all other limbs and body parts. The cranium encapsulates and contains the brain. This area could be called the crown of man; as its placement is above all (other anatomical parts). The head is a crowning component of the human species.

The sefira of keser which means "crown" is situated above, and acts as the "head "of the all the other sefiros. As such, keser radiates its light & energizes all the sefiros below it. One aspect of keser is related to the outer expression of G-d's will. Keser from a humanistic, psycho-spiritual perspective is linked to the human will and soul powers, which too gives the animative drive; energy to all other aspects of a human being.

Rosh Hashanah, "the head of the year" is time when we coronate/crown the King of the universe. We crown G-d in order that we be crowned in our own lives for a new year of health, happiness, prosperity, peace and furthermore to be judged meritoriously.

The new year also affords a new life so to speak. As Jews we can shed the impediments and negativity from our so called crown/brain (feelings, thoughts and actions) and become something new.

Shedding our former self to reveal a new self for the New Year! Generating new mochin (brains) and with it a new set of thoughts, feelings and actions. This transformative process can be analogous to shedding skin both externally and internally. The inner self (thoughts & feelings) morphs and effectuates change to the outer self (actions).

By shedding old, inoperative, non-productive ways & thought patterns you emancipate yourself from the past residue. This "shedding" brings to light the revelatory beauty of the new year and a new life! Leaving behind your former self and becoming invigorated as a new self (or more selfless). This is a process like molting that is woven into the nature of Rosh Hashanah By coronating Hashem and shedding the past years "skin" that enables us to use the upcoming New Year in a new way, in rich alignment with G-d.

Interestingly, the Hebrew word for skin is "ohr" (spelled with ayin) and Hebrew word for light is "ohr"(spelled with alef) and both are pronounced the same. One angle on this might be by shedding our old "skin" gives us new opportunities to shine with a new light from the inside out. The Torah is the orah (Light) for external, internal and eternal life. As Rabbi Hillel said, "More flesh, more worms… More Torah, more Life."

With awareness, accountability & action we can ring in the New Year with vibrancy and bring fresh light into our hearts, minds and souls.

Use the New Year as a springboard to new things. A new you. A clean slate. Let this be a crowning achievement. A head above the rest. By "shedding skin" it reveals a new light within so we can begin again.

21

Soular Eclipse

An eclipse is a durational obscurity relating to an astronomical episode by a passing shadow, body or object.

On a rapacious and expansionary planet it is paramount to take stock of the atmosphere in which we choose to orbit in. The gravitational pull of what so often surrounds us can frequently engulf us and "what we own, ends up owning us." The shadows of opaque physicality in the world can project an eclipse on the soul.

Rabbi Avraham Greenbaum expounds on a selection from Rebbe Nachman's magnum opus Likutey Moharan 1:133- The sun radiates continuously with equal intensity at the opening and middle of the day. What obstructs the sun is only the earth, which intervenes between man and the sun. Due to the position of the earth, the light spreads progressively as the day begins but steadily increases until it spreads over the earth.

Likewise, the radiance of Torah shines incessantly while

the obstruction is on the side of the receivers. The cause of the barrier is the intervening "earth" – the material world. People are so profoundly sunk in the material world that they are unable to receive the light of G-d and His Torah. The Torah is enormously great and expansive but a tiny handbreadth – this world- stands before people's eyes, preventing them from seeing the light of the Torah despite the fact that the world is microscopic in contrast.

How could something so diminutive block something a thousand times more colossal?

To comprehend this, reflect on how a small coin held in front of your eyes can prevent you from seeing a grand mountain countless times larger than the minuscule coin. However, because the coin is directly in front of your eyes, it blocks your total field of vision.

In the same manner, when a person enters the physical world, he remains sunk in the vanities of the world and imagines that there is nothing better. This minute insignificant world stands in his way, preventing him from seeing the marvelous light of the Torah. This is precisely equivalent to the way the immense light of the sun is blocked by the intervening earth even though the sun is many times larger than the earth.

In any event, if one removes the infinitesimal barrier from one's eyes- averting one's eyes from this world and instead elevating one's head and lifting one's eyes beyond the intervening world- one attains a view of the great amazing light of the Torah. For the Torah's luminosity is far greater than all of this world and its vanities. It's just that the world stands before people's eyes and does not sanction them to lift their eyes upward and absorb the light of the Torah. It's akin to the small coin in front of the eyes that prevents one from seeing the great mountain.

Many stand in their own shadow and wonder why it's dark.

Rabbi Freifeld, zt"l asks, "Can anyone possibly think that there is any light in the world other than the light that shines out from the Torah?" He goes on to purport that attaining wisdom through the lodestar of Torah is the key. He continues, "You try your hardest, and if you can not penetrate to the answer, you have to pray to the Almighty to remove the cobwebs from your eyes and your brain, to cleanse your mind of all that blurs the clarity of your vision and thought. It's all up to you. If you ask for it, G-d will give it to you." Shedding the umbra and eclipsing impediments we take on a new light; "One opens his eyes, and the first thing that goes through his mind is that he is an immortal being, a spark of the divine en route to the next world, the eternal world, that he has to use everyday to accomplish and achieve something. How different he will feel when he gets out of bed with a buoyant heart and a spring in his step, how hopeful and encouraged by the greatness of the enterprise of his existence." Insomuch as a shadow can only be cast with the presence of light...And light has been called "the symbol of truth." Torah, "orah"- light.

The extraterrestrial unfolds as the shadows of physicality

intersect with the surface of the soul. The obstacles can either be used in conjunction with growth or opposition; in prograde or retrograde motion. The celestial mechanics must be *soul*ar powered. Driven by soular energy and propelled by soular winds- the winds of Sinai. The soular gusts diminish the ecliptic orbital plane and give credence to soular panels which attract the light of the Torah. We elevated the nadir by stretching beyond our so called nature. Soaring to new heights to reach the zenith through proper alignment & spirit*jew*ality we orchestrate cosmic harmony. The sky's the limit as we shuttle within our soular system; to move from a soular eclipse to G-d's sole proprietorship.

22

Architect of Light

בְּרֵאשִׁית, Bereishis is the first Hebrew word in the Torah and it means, "in the beginning." However, when probing deeper the same Hebrew letters can be rearranged to spell/ read רֹאשׁ בַּיִת, Rosh Bayis which means, "Head of house" indicating and conveying that Hashem is the Rosh Bayis of the entire "house", i.e. the Universe. Hashem is the master architect and builder, the physical and spiritual designer of the vast expanse of creation. Also notably, Bereishis בְּרֵאשִׁית can be rearranged to form the words בְּרִית אֵשׁ, "Covenant of Fire", and again, בְּרֵאשִׁית can be rearranged to form the words אֵשׁ רַבָּתִי, "great fire", a reference both to the Torah itself and how it was given. Rabbi D. Sutton shared the Zohar alludes to בראשית, the opening word of the Torah, contains the same letters as ירא שבת — "awe of Shabbos." Shabbos is integrally bound to yiras Shamayim, and thus the higher we elevate our standards of yiras Shamayim, the more we can feel and experience the kedusha (holiness) of Shabbos. The Vilna

Gaon and other Torah luminaries divulged בְּרֵאשִׁית, "in the beginning", encodes all potentiality.

We have an opportunity to co-partner with Hashem in the continual construction of the world. In connecting to the light of the first day of Creation, which is Chesed (Kindness) we too become molders and builders of light. Utilizing the tools found in our Torah toolbox; tefillos, mitzvos and working to refine our character traits assist in sculpting the world both microcosmically and macrocosmically.

Construction worker or destruction worker? It's your choice.

With agile persistence we're able to navigate this fragile existence. Through this process we labor to reclaim our mind and soul from the vacuous cultural engineers. As clearly expressed by our own venerated Rabbi Slatus in Savannah, "happiness and success are based on the realization and knowledge the whatever you may have should be used appropriately." Using the world appropriately is key in constructing an abode where the Divine Presence can dwell.

Architecturally we are afforded the ability to construct the world with G-d if we implement the correct tools and faculties.

The Zohar illuminates, "As we correct and transform, we reveal a measure of hidden light in direct proportion to the degree of inner change we've undergone. It is this spiritual change that expands our internal vessel, allowing us to receive a greater portion of hidden light." By electing to be construction workers and architects of light we are able to build. And what we build ends up building us. The Zohar continues, "No matter how far one may fall spiritually, the Light of the Creator is always present the moment we decide to rise above our negativity."

As such we must choose to compose a life of light. "The essence of free will is to choose to be a soul, not a body. The battle is to do what your soul wants, not what your body feels like doing" relates Rabbi Noah Weinberg. Channeling the proclivities to be constructive becomes the soul work that manufactures a healthy house and milieu.

Rabbi Akiva observed, if a rock, though extremely hard, can be hollowed out by water, how much more so should it be possible for The Light, which is compared to water, to change my heart. I will begin to study it, and try to become a scholar of The Light. A erudite mystic once said, "Once we were particles of Light, now we are beings of Light, radiating love." Bestow light and compassion on the world and see that energy returned to you.

In a very deep way everything that exists in the entire universe is light materialized.

Let's work to follow the blueprints and framework set out in the Torah. The Rosh Bayis (Hashem) has supplied and infused us with the necessary instructions. "Let there be light!" Let us be light! Israelites = Israe*lights*. Let's build together to perpetually create a world which facilitates a dwelling place for the light of Hashem. In this capacity, we co-create and engineer a blazing covenantal relationship, "in the beginning" with the Rosh Bayis.

23

Slave to Freedom

Everyone is a slave. We're all slaves in one capacity or another. If so, where does slavery end & freedom begin? Or can slavery and freedom co-exist harmoniously in a meaningful, transcendental manner?

Some maintain that liberation is found in "freeing" your body and mind; doing whatever you feel anytime you feel like doing it. Yet, any perspicacious mind & eye can see that creates a pseudo sense of freedom and is the basest, most empty avenue of slavery. Slaves to social constructs, money, media, politics, trends, every passion and the like only further magnifies that some are led & fed like mindless sheep. They feel so "free" (and typically end up judging and putting down others that differ) however in truth, they're often the most enslaved without even realizing it. So enveloped and self absorbed they lack insight. A servant to their emotions. This is where perceived freedom is really slavery. This minutia of pettiness gives a false sense of freedom rendering one ineffectual and enfeebled.

In stark contrast, there's a slavery which is uniquely linked to authentic freedom. This sort of emancipatory equation is revealed and animated during Passover. Its story is the story of our lives as Jews. Redeemed and freed as slaves in Egypt, and ultimately rectified in servitude to G-d. Freed from man-made slavery and renewed as an eved (servant) of Hashem. To move from a galus to geulah in thought, speech and deed is where we unlock the redemption seeds.

Rabbi Freeman, "The biblical slavery of Egypt represents bondage to your own self. Every day, every moment, must be an exodus from the self. If you're not leaving Egypt, you're already back there." Don't be incarcerated by your past. It was a lesson, not a life sentence.

Rabbi Moshe Chaim Luzzatto explains the redemptive effects the Exodus had on the Jews at that time and on each of us contemporaneously: Via the Exodus from Egypt, Klal Yisrael was chosen and separated from all others. On the first night of Pesach there is a renewal in which the rectifications of the original first Pesach in Egypt are reawakened. Every year on this particular night every participatory member of the Seder is again elevated beyond the ordinary terrestrial state of humankind. This annual process also assists in the diminishment of the dross physicality which we're so often saturated in. Again, as we revisit the night of the 15th of Nissan the mitzvos we perform generates the tikun that takes place on Passover; a true expression of freedom.

Rabbi Naftali Reich shares, "Our sages share with us that the central theme of our Rosh Hashana avodah centers on malchiyus … coronating Hashem as king of the universe and king over ourselves. This concept is somewhat hard for us to digest. After all, the idea of a Monarch, invested with imperial powers, runs counter to all that our society values. Our democratic mind set screams for equal rights and a fair judicial system. The concept of slavery and servitude is also an anathema to societies "progressive" thought process. We, however, understand and appreciate that surrendering to a higher authority is the key to joy and true liberty."

From slavery to freedom to what we may take liberty to call "slavedom", which equates to a deeper more meaningful slavery of sorts in service to a Higher Power and calling. This form of "slavery" is the most freeing. This is where perceived slavery is really freedom. Newly released from the shackles of sick societal standards we have the opportunity to soar. No longer strictly bound by the physical dimensions we are able to connect ourselves, our souls in service to G-d. Abolishment to manifest our destiny on a body, mind and soul level. Know that life is the time that Hashem gives us to figure out how we are going to spend eternity.

True freedom is found in spiritual custody. It's the apex of Pesach where this brand of slavery & freedom merge and each of us has a unique opportunity to break the chains and capitulate to the Master of the universe.

24

Divided We Stand, United We Fall

Politics is defined as, "the art and science of administration and government."

Campaigns and electioneering are in full swing. Filtering through the so called facts and trends can be daunting and polarizing. History has been proven be "his" or "hiss" story with a host of antagonists playing the role of, sleazy slippery slimy snakes simply slandering & slithering stealthily in a swarming swamp of swindlers. As such, lies become truths, facts become fiction and we are left to decide which direction to cast our vote. Platforms are underpinned by feeble foundations and profanations. In a sense it has become a "profane"nation, a demockracy. Some people are so caught up in politics they forgot about humanity. Take a stand, but try not to lose balance in the process. It's no wonder we're ripped and torn asunder. A mass astringent may be needed to halt the multiple hemorrhaging. Divided we stand, united we fall.

In a macrocosmic fashion, Washington is washing-tons

of fabrications and manipulations as we sleep. Much of it guised as "promises " (pro-misses). See the crisp, clean laundry being hung out to dry over night. Unconscionable conduct, incorrigibly bellicose on all sides. Intoxicated by their own self importance they trudge on mired in controversy. Pervading and parading in this process are often pugnacious politicians crusading and vigorously campaigning for their special interests. Meanwhile, many of the propagandizing pundits scurry to clean the mess with their intellectual confections. The gall of it all. This air of arrogance needs to be fumigated. Breaking news! The news is broken.

It's interesting how the word "politics" is made up of the words "poli" meaning "many" in Latin, and "tics" as in "bloodsucking creatures." In the meantime, the clock is what's really ticking. So divisive. Cherry-picking. Lock-stepping. Sloganeering. Prattling. Lampooning. And we all pretend like we really know what is going on. Right? I cast a vote in opposition to that thought. Intelligence, humility and compassion annuls hubris, mudslinging and malice. M. Twain said, "Politicians and diapers must be changed often, and for the same reason."

Ideally it should be for the betterment of all mankind; not the betterment of only my kind. Each of us can have diverse viewpoints and opinions while campaigning to remain civil and considerate. In the battleground state(s) of mind stand strong for what you believe as you exercise your free will. Electing to live your own life is important, but to have some degree of objectivity sponsors and endorses a more truthful exit poll.

Rabbi Eliyahu Dessler said, anyone who has prejudices and whose perceptions are colored by self-interest will never see the truth in any area in which his bias operates. Only when his bias is removed will he be able to understand the truth.

What comes out of the mouths of many politicians is the leading cause of truth decay. Most politicians, sad to say, are well-versed prevaricators. The truth is, "Most people don't really want the truth; they just want a constant reassurance that what they believe is the truth." Everyone has their own slant on the way to bending the truth.

A Yiddish proverb sets the record straight, "If each one sweeps before his own door, the whole street is clean."

It's been promulgated, "In the civil society, the individual is recognized and accepted as more than an abstract statistic or faceless member of some group; rather, he is a unique, spiritual being with a soul and a conscience. He is free to discover his own potential and pursue his own legitimate interests, tempered, however, by a moral order that has its foundation in faith and guides his life and all human life through the prudent exercise of judgment."

Here stands the current state of affairs: As Americans we stand propped on the threshold; walking a fine line between hope and dire straits. It is valuable to consider our role as Jews in this all. Conviction of policy and the like are nice but what is the Emes (Truth)? The true Emes is not found wafting around the corridors of Washington or in the halls of academia. Even the great framers and redactors of the Constitution did not have the unadulterated Emes. The Emes is found in the Torah. No lobbyist, no camera angles, no platforms, teleprompters, red or blue states called for. "The truth is still the truth even if no one believes it. A lie is still a lie, even if everyone believes it." Cease obfuscating the truth with typical hyperbolic political statements.

The Truth has no agenda.

The Sfas Emes sways the Electoral College with his penetrating insights: "The concept of the "years head" is an allusion to the rejuvenation of the Jewish people." He continues, "the name Yisrael (Israel) re-arranged spells "Li Rosh" or "Israel is my head." Every Rosh Hashana, Israel is designated by Hashem to head and lead humankind which renews its rapport with Hashem. Furthermore, the concept of leading is not accomplished by an independent and divided existence. Rather we must be the first; the head of humankind to adhere to Hashem Who is the true Rosh (Head). The renewal of Israel, humankinds head is also a time for the restoration and reinstatement of the soul. Our mission in the universe is allied to that of the soul and body- to infuse a lifeless void with spiritual life and vitality."

We should try not to be merely defined by an abbreviation: D, R, I or any political party affiliation. Consider this pithy saying, "what if I told you that the left wing and the right wing belong to the same bird." It's been noted: "Politics: A strife of interests masquerading as a contest of principles. The conduct of public affairs for private advantage." Also, be careful not to dehumanize people you disagree with; because in our self-righteousness, we can easily exhibit the same behaviors we have such a distaste for in others. Let's aim to put people over party. Humanity is greater than status. We are more than this, and there is so much more to life. We're always stronger united than we are divided. We need to stop filibustering our lives away.

Civil-eyes see civi*lies*.

We are all *flaw*makers. Our bill of rights and wrongs are held up before the Celestial Cabinet. A close accounting and system of checks and balances makes for a closer encounter. This is a spiritual bailout opportunity for all of us in the general assembly.

Don't be apathetic. Do your part. Please vote, don't gloat. Don't allow the outcome to totally dictate your life. Be steeled in faith and you'll be more settled. Understand, after voting and putting in earnest effort, whatever the result, it's ultimately from Hashem.

We are ambassadors, emissaries of the Infinite. Let's act accordingly. In this we can ensure a landslide victory for all. No need for a recount.

This may not necessarily win the popular vote, but this should be our one true affiliation. Keep at the forefront whose Administration is governing and running the world; the congress of Emes. In this House and Senate there is no stonewalling, as G-d is the One and only Executive, Judicial and Legislative branch on which the whole universe stands. In G-d we trust- the united state(s) of body, mind and soul.

It's the government of the covenant. The court of the Supreme. This is the *awe*fice we should show the most reverence.

G-d bless America… G-d has blessed America, now it's time for America to bless G-d.

25

Our Soul Duty

The Shechinah has been in exile since the highest sparks fell to the lower realms, and more physically speaking since the Temples destruction. Much of this is due to our thoughts, speech and actions. It's our soul duty to emancipate the Divine Presence from captivity.

The task of human beings is to search for these lost sparks, elevate them by identifying them as divine sparks, and by doing so help to restore unity to the world. All people have the ability to elevate the sparks that are connected to the root of their souls. Whenever they redeem the sparks that belong to their soul-roots, the sparks come together to form a great light that expresses our partnership in Tikkun Olam — improving the world.

Every day, at every moment there needs to be a constant flow of energy and vitality.

Rabbi Shepherd teaches, "Every good deed we do especially when combined with the right thoughts, intentions and prayers elevates the Shechina one level after another. When the Shechinah will return to its place there is a constant everlasting unity. This is the redemption when everything returns to its original place, and the system reaches its fullest potential; the gateway for the revelation we wait for every moment."

When Hashem wants us to grow, He takes us out of our comfort zone.

Our being mesakein the Shechinah according to the Ramak in Tomer Devorah: The yetzer hara should be bound and sculpted, in that, all physical desires and anger should be directed towards sweetening the gevuros (power, severities) by providing for one's wife. One should say, "by providing, I'm bringing restoration to the Shechinah." The Ramak goes onto divulge all household necessities restore the Shechinah by re-channeling physical desire and sweeting the yetzer hara to fulfill the Divine Will. Therefore, one should bend his yetzer hara to the positive and arouse it to restore the Divine Presence and subsequently concentrate on sweetening all those acts of restoring the Shechinah with his yetzer tov (positive inclination) via Chesed/Tiferes from the Right. This states the Ramak is for the sake of the Supernal Union by sweetening the judgements on the Left and rectifying them through kindness & mercy on the Right. This prescription from the Ramak is activated by how one molds his yetzer hara (negative inclination) to benefit his comparable helpmate Hashem has chosen. Practically, by treating our significant other better we are doing the holy work of restoring the

Divine Presence. Seeking and creating shalom with others is a restoration & rectification and when one returns to it all back at it soul root Source that is called teshuvah (return). It's revealed in the hebrew word teshuv by adding a H(ey) to manifest teshuvah and in this process we return the final (H)ey to the YHVH.

The Zohar teaches that teshuvah also energizes the Shechinah and continues, believe not that man consists solely of flesh, skin, bones, and veins. The real part of man is his soul, and the things just mentioned, the skin, flesh, bones, and veins, are only an outward covering, a veil, but are not the man. When man departs he divests himself of all the veils which cover him. And these different parts of our body correspond to the secrets of the Divine wisdom. The skin typifies the heavens which extend everywhere and cover everything like a garment. The flesh puts us in mind of the evil side of the universe. The bones and the veins symbolize the Divine chariot, the inner powers of man which are the servants of G-d. But they are all but an outer covering. For, inside man, there is the secret of the Heavenly Man. . . . Everything below takes place in the same manner as everything above. This is the meaning of the remark that G-d created man in His own image. But just as in the heavens, which cover the whole universe, we behold different shapes brought about by the stars and the planets to teach us concerning hidden things and deep secrets, so upon the skin which covers our body there are shapes and forms which are like planets and stars to our bodies. All these shapes have a hidden meaning.

Everything has a some sort of interlocking relationship and purpose.

Rabbi Yitzchak Luria (Arizal) related, The person to whom our Torah speaks is neither a man nor a woman, but both combined. For this is how Adam was first created and this is how we are in essence: Two half-bodies that are truly one. The minds are two, but the bodies, the souls and the very core of these two people are one and the same. This is why the character and responsibilities of a man and a woman differ, for each side of the body does its part to compliment the other. The Ari continues, the Talmud teaches that since the destruction G-d sits and makes matches. The simple explanation is that He puts couples together in marriage. Even deeper, this helps raise the fallen sparks out of the sitra achra, in order to couple them each with the soul they belong to. Each one of the couple is actually a lost, fallen soul portion relative to the other. Therefore the Talmud calls finding a mate like looking for a lost article.

Rav Chaim Shmulevitz taught when Hashem declared, "it's not good for man to be alone," it means because he needs to be afforded the ability to make peace and help others. This can be learned from the word in the plural for life, chaim, to indicate a lesson that all of existence is predicated upon the ability to act kindly and with consideration toward others.

Two must strive to work as one to fuse with Holy One. This is the secret of elevating the feminine waters to connect with masculine waters to make unification of Light and vessel. Taking the light and putting it into vessels to improve ourselves and the world is of the essence. The ultimate tikun (rectification) is to harmoniously connect to the Infinite, yet remain in a finite world. Restoring the Shechinah (Divine Presence) is a part of this process by seeking peace with others, learning Torah and observing the mitzvos in thought, speech and action is to be a spiritual tactician. We have a unique mission to bring unity and fill the world with a "global, human consciousness of the Light of Hashem." This is a soul goal. It's not just our sole duty, it's our soul duty.

26

Spaced In

*****Space*****noun, often attributive \\'spās\: the amount of an area, room, surface, etc., that is empty or available for use: an area that is used or available for a specific purpose: an empty area between things (Websters Dictionary).

Space is qualitative and quantitatively important. What fills in the "space" between our seconds, minutes, hours, days, weeks, months and years makes up the sum total of our lives. What we elect, via free will, to launch and color our days with ultimately will determine the various hues, tones, constellations and destinations that make up life as we know it.

Just as, if not more paramount , is what colors in the space between the human psyche. Rabbi Aryeh Carmell shared as Rav Dessler revealed in Strive for Truth!, "there is a vast empty space in the human psyche, situated between intellectual knowledge and its realizations of the heart." As soon as there is a chasm between the "knowledge and heart" the inclination(evil/negative) entrenches itself in the resulting vacuum and access is permitted to all the yearnings and imaginings of this world." He continues, "only when one achieves a close association of "knowledge" and "heart", with no gulf in between, will a person's actions accord with his knowledge."

The space between "knowledge" and "heart" is the coliseum where the war with the yetzer is held and the place where free will is exercised. Rav Dessler elicits and implores, "our chief goal should be to capture this space." By capturing the space, potential prospects bloom for all moral adjudications. The epicenter of phrenic, cerebral and visceral life now can be outlined as follows: "knowledge"—— "the space" (free will is exercised/the yetzers battleground) ——"heart." How to conquer this space? How to bridge and meld "knowledge" and "heart." How to fill this mental lacuna?

Vanquishment and/or holy expansion of this space is utterly and wholly challenging. It takes great effort and intellectual fortitude; plus, untainted honesty to conquer "the space." Discipline from the mental, emotional and behavioral hippodromes are all at play in taking ownership of "the space."

Orbiting and injecting wisdom by dint of the Torah and its encompassing spirituality, the empty mental space is suffused with sagacity. Consequently, over time, the yetzer hara is swept and cleared from the empty space and now can be bridged, filled or expanded with sanctity; as the evil inclination no longer rents "space", the darkness is diminished by light.

Be the light from one orbit to the next *ohr*bit.

This locale of the inner (space) life impacts and imparts spiritual and behavioral health to the outer (space) life. This concept is truly mind expanding when given thought and full respect. The broad expanse of this "space" concept by Rav Dessler infuses the mind with sapient, intellectual ornamentation and beautification.

Let's begin to integrate this mussar into our lives. All systems go on full throttle through new atmospheres of the mind on this self controlled "space" ship; sky rocketing to a new "space" stations in life. Space cadets no more. Untie the astro-knots to escape the gravitational pull of the yetzer hara (negative inclinations) & to reside on a better planet (plan-it).

While occupying space in this world we should be aware that spiritual development leads to awareness, wisdom and transformation. Stay spaced in, not spaced out.

27

Panicdemic

"Calm breeds calm. Panic breeds panic."

It seems the pandemic has mutated into a full blown *panic*demic.

Is this herd immunity or heard immunity? Herd impunity is more like it. To mask or not to mask? Let's call a spade a spade, the "masks" everyone has been wearing long before COVID-19 should be considered. You know what I'm talking about. That "mask" we all hide behind from time to time. None of us are exempt or immune from that disease no matter how much sheltering in place. So much "masking" tape and selfish adhesives working overtime to hold the fragmentations, manipulations and anxieties together. Maybe some masks we should be endeavoring to take off, while others we should put on. I don't know. But, I do know, "In a world where everyone wears a mask, it's a privilege to see a soul." Unmask the blessings in disguise.

Breathe. Calm. Connect.

Life is a balance of holding on and letting go, shared a wise mystic. Of course, there are rational precautionary measures that should be implemented and followed. Think of others too through this process. Rabbi Sharga Silverstein was quoted as saying, "Let us think less of what the future will bring us and more of what we will bring the future." Let's strive to unify for the greater good instead of allowing the viral divisive media and droplets of the yetzer hara (negative inclinations) to reign supreme.

Me or we? Virus or us? Vir*us*. It's us, no matter how you slice it. Mortality and morality.

There's another type of pandemic; the pandemic of the mind, which is a self-imposed brain event. To mitgate its pervasive effects we should understand, "the fears we don't face become our limits."

Here too is where a steady dose of emunah (faith) could be injected daily to stave off the deeply embedded psychological infectious diseases. Due diligence in conjunction with emunah is the way. This plus wisdom is a balm of calm, a vaccine of sorts.

Superimposition and irrational fear is not a healthy approach psychologically, physically &/or spiritually. To live with that type of "mask" is smothering on so many levels to so many people. Fear mongering and judgment comes from the sitra achra (other side). One lesson Hashem may be trying to teach us from the coronavirus is that we should be unifying and not in discordance with one another. Let's be safe and stay sound together.

Know, there is a deeper unity effervescing to the surface.

The Midrash says, Man enters the world with closed hands, as if to say, "The world is mine"; he leaves with open hands, as if to say, "I take nothing with me."

Come out of spiritual lockdown.

Get vaccinated with emunah (faith) and let it be our shield and sword along with common sense. Be guided by faith, intelligence, vigilance and passion. If you truly believe that Hashem is in control of everything then you'll be able to let most things go after putting in hishtadlus (personal effort). This is not related to seasonality and elective community immunity.

Hopefully the next pandemic will be shalom (peace) and may it spread like wildfire.

Stay grounded. Calm breeds calm. Faith defeats fear.

28

—

Of Air & Ear

Song: A melody sung or played with musical instruments.

What is the architecture of song? A song is assembled on a variation of seven notes in an arrangement. These seven notes can be melded into innumerable combinations. A song is a vibration of sound waves collected and processed by the ears. The processed sound then dispatches signals to the brain. The brain processes the signals of song. The development is a composition of instruments and expression that delivers an auditory spectrum upon entrance to the recipient's ear(s). Hearing is a complex process which is a fundamentally automatic, passive activity. Listening consists of discerning various meanings and messages of the sound waves which is a more active process.

Song remains a blend of musical textures: A sound sculpture. Layers of sonic energy that paint the canvas of air and ear. The evocative nature of song can have an influence and impact both mentally and physically. Nevertheless the profundity of song is its ability to transport and stir the mind, heart and soul from the perspective of the giver (composer) and receiver (listener). From air to ear song is a mutual symbiotic relationship of sorts; a sublime apparitional dance of frequency and timbre.

The Concert by the Sea: Parshas B'Shalach is called Shabbos Shirah because it contains the song sung by the Jews following the splitting of the Red Sea. A song of untainted faith; a tidal sound wave cresting in crescendo. The fusion of sound in the Shirah endorsed no distortion or dissonance. Rather it was melodious and harmonious. Commencing at the dramatic departure from Egypt, capturing the theatrical aquatic display, and onto its heart-pounding, sensational finish; the Shirah is a musical score measuring cacophony to symphony; a swirling soundscape of rhythm, pitch and volume parading on the brim of and parachuting off of each note.

Rabbi Israel ben Eliezer said, "You must know that everything depends on you. That with your every mitzvah, the universe resonates in blissful harmony that heals and nurtures. That with a single negative act, the entire cosmic symphony falls apart."

If your life is stuck skipping in a negative groove lift the stylus and change the tune.

The audible is clear: Just as the ears assist in maintaining equilibrium so too the Shirah of this and every Shabbos aids in symmetry and equipoise. Hashem conducts the orchestra in this mortal amphitheater and each of us is a note in the enduring song of life. All the unique layers of instrumentation discernible and uplifting. A shirah is a soundtrack like no other. Can you hear the resonance in every soul? No Grammy, Solid Gold Hit, Oldie but Goodie or Billboard Top 100 has ever ridden the airwaves like this genre breaking Shirah (song). Presented in high-depth surround sound: Hear, O Israel... Listen, O Israel.

29

Cosmospolitan

I dare you to think outside the box. The box being the abstract confines that seems to fasten each of us to our so called "lifestyles." No one escapes the margins and precincts that they have selected or that have befallen them.

Rabbi Freifeld ztz"l explains, out of weakness, lassitude or insecurity, people glance at others, at other groups, at other classes, and seek to follow their lead. For some raison d'être they believe that the treasure is in other hands and that their own hands are vacant.

He continues, "Human intelligence, it seems to me has just about played itself out. So many attempts at forming the perfect society have been made throughout the ages. We've had everything- autocracy, oligarchy, democracy, fascism, socialism, communism- nothing has brought peace and happiness to humankind. None of them work as it was meant to work. If a system helps in one area, it fails in another. A patch here, a leak there. That's what everything is-patchwork. And this is true in all fields of human inquiry and endeavor. All is patchwork, glorified patchwork."

Is there an "ism" that is not? Is there a spiritual reality that offers transcendence beyond the systematic patchworks?

The Shem Mishmuel delivers from the Arizal an outstanding concept; stating that the Exodus from Mitzrayim can be equated to childbirth. The pangs of labor intensify until the actual birth looms, so too the plagues intensified and out of the pangs was birthed the distinct nation of Israel. Diamonds are made under pressure. And hence, a diamond was born.

The treasures are honed and mined outside the box and within the context of authentic spirituality. Each sparkling jewel resides in the heart of the individual. Shop around; you won't discover anything more inestimable and authentic than the chic and elegant gems collected from the gleaming lights of the Torah! Each of us is a unique priceless gem in the crown of creation. A coronation of the Most High and consequently special amongst the cosmos. Multi-celestial sophisticates. True galactic *cosmos*politans. Israel is real and the Torah is the eternal deed to the land of Israel.

Regardless of how one measures against others; the fine clarity, color, cut and carat adorns the cosmos with a resplendent magnificence that gives birth and creditability to acquire daily compliments from Heaven.

30

Any Given Shabbos

Time-out!

It's Friday, the sun has dipped below the horizon. The Divine Presence (Shechinah) is radiating and illuminating the terrestrial stadium (Olam Ha-Zeh). Six week(weak)days have passed. Now strength and the scent of freshly drawn lines inundates the atmosphere. A clear discernible separation between the holy and mundane becomes increasingly more palpable. The field is groomed for and engaged in the sport of prayer and learning. The crowd (malachim-angels) has gathered in record attendance. There are new formations in this arena as Jews scramble to make forward progress. It's Shabbos! The Supernal Bowl!

Please give your undivided attention for our national anthem: Shema Yisrael.

Our One and only Coach and all around universal-QB (G-d) is undefeated and has had home field advantage eternally. Kickoff time is…well, that has long begun…

As Jews we have won the toss! Do you choose to receive the ball and our play book, the Torah on this gridiron of life? The audible(s) have been called: 248...365...613...Hut! Hut! It's your move. Keep your eye on the ball because the Yetzer Hara (YH) may try to draw you offsides; to the other side (sitra achra). A turnover can change the outcome. An occasional fumble or encroachment can however be rectified and capitalized on with teshuvah. Stepping out of bounds on this astro-turf does not stop the clock. Life continues; it is a one possession game with no overtime. Rebbe Nachman of Breslov offers from his playbook: "Life is a narrow bridge; the main thing is to not be afraid." Life is a goal-line stand. Pay attention to the clarion call. Choosing the proper routes and breaking tackles translates into more yardage (mitzvos). Stay connected to the offensive and defensive coordinators the Chachamim and Rabbeim. Staying linked to the aforementioned aids in anticipating the YH if it goes into zone or man to man coverage or is charged with a string of penalties, personal fouls/unnecessary roughness. Time of possession and controlling the clock is paramount on the gridiron of life. First and goal:

The strategy is clear; the objective known; play prevent defense against the YH minimizing penetration while you simultaneously generate more yardage offensively. Avoid the blitz and interceptions from outside influences that have a tendency to sack and take away the best of intentions. The yetzer hara has field position only if you give it. Tackle the

YH before it gets to you. Keep your helmet (head), heart and soul in the game.

TGIS (Thank G-d it's Shabbos)!

Stay observant and on the ball.

As Jews we became first round draft picks at Mt. Sinai for the privileged NFL (National Frum League). Know your heritage. Know now is the time to come off the sidelines and bench and join the team. All endorsements and commercials aside; the play clock is ticking. Your number has been called. Suit up and play. The Supernal Bowl is not annually, it is weekly. On Shabbos there are four quarters: the first quarter is Friday night Kabbalas Shabbos/Maariv. The second quarter is Shacharis. Score a TD with a DT (D'var Torah)! Halftime is sponsored by the refreshing and ever quenching Shabbos menucha (rest). The third quarter is Mincha. The fourth quarter is Shalosh Seudos.

Avoid the rush and score the winning touchdown in the Supernal Bowl with Hashem on any given Shabbos! Become G-d's number one receiver and you will unquestionably beat the odds and reach the end zone (Olam Haba)!

31

Elements on the Periodic Table of Life

Everything I am not, made me everything I am.

The things we do or don't do make up our lives and make us who are. Time may fly, but we can be the pilot. So, to get from point A to B we got to C (see) it through. A little momentum goes a long way. Proactivity produces productivity.

Learning to blend, balance and adapt to the various elements (be it solid, liquid or gas) on the periodic table of life is crucial. We can either be a chemical reaction or chemical pro-action; proactive or reactive. One's disposition often determines ones position and ability to deal with transitions, and to manage the relationship between self and others. Moreover, to be okay if it happens and okay if it doesn't happen is a powerfully peaceful place to be. Try to live there. Flexibility, empathy and creativity should be fused to manufacture substantial outcomes.

We are all here for a short period of time, only periodically.

We are compounded part-time particles. To set the periodic table to effectuate healthier relationships between the various element properties, and also to improve behaviours of undiscovered or newly synthesized elements in life may be an atomic undertaking. Nevertheless, our interactions can go beyond symbols, status and numbing numbers. Formulating a more meaningful life through better chemistry with self, others and Hashem can be done. Be consistent, not conditional.

The Baal Shem Tov said, "Alas! the world is full of enormous lights and mysteries, and man shuts them from himself with one small hand!" Open your eyes to the hand of the Knower of all mysteries. Microscope the spiritual molecular structure that binds it all. Seek that knowledge and let it generate a positive chain reaction.

When knowledge acts as *gnaw*ledge it chews at us to learn more and respond in accordance. Know this, you can lead people to knowledge but you can't make them think. Think about the way we act & interact with ourselves and each other. The Chofetz Chaim wrote in his Sefer Shmiras Haloshon, "The way in which one acts towards others determines the way in which Heaven will act towards him...As our Sages state "Whoever has compassion towards others will be shown compassion from Above" (Shabbos 151b); and "Whoever refrains from exacting his measure [of retribution from others for the wrong they caused him] will have all his sins forgiven (Rosh Hashana 17a)."

Some have scant regard for others. Be of substance. Be sure

also to encourage your friends not to become disheartened, no matter what happens. You may be all too aware of your own failings, but this should not prevent you from encouraging others. It is easier to inspire others than to strengthen yourself, for "A prisoner cannot free himself," disclosed Rebbe Nachman. Rather than breaking each other down, let's build each other up. Rabbi Hirsch adds, "If someone is too tired to give you a smile, leave one of your own, because no one needs a smile as much as those who have none to give."

Albert Einstein shared, "A human being is part of a whole, called by us the 'Universe' a part limited in time and space. He experiences himself, his thoughts, and feelings, as something separated from the rest a kind of optical delusion of his consciousness. This delusion is a kind of prison for us, restricting us to our personal desires and to affection for a few persons nearest us. Our task must be to free ourselves from this prison by widening our circles of compassion to embrace all living creatures and the whole of nature in its beauty."

Disembark from negativity. Be protonic. At the nucleus drive to be a stable, positive charged proton, not a "negatron." Understand, "People are like stained-glass windows. They sparkle and shine when the sun is out, but when the darkness sets in, their true beauty is revealed only if there is a light from within."

The way we treat each other makes us who we are. Rav Avraham Yitzchak Kook noted, "The love of G-d's creatures must include all humankind, regardless of religion and race.

The narrow mindedness that sees whatever is outside our people as impure and contaminated is one of those terrible blights that destroys any good building/structure." When we choose the positive over the negative, the selfless over the selfish we become more. It makes us better able to weather, interact & meld the elements on the periodic table of life. Don't Dv8. Cre8. Oxygenate. 8 is the atomic number of Oxygen and represents of infinity.

"Olam Chesed Yibaneh…" (Psalm 89:3) – the world is built on kindness. The power of chesed is part of the inner architecture of the universe. The properties of kindness should be used on all of the elements interactively, both individually and with others. The elemental building blocks of chesed (kindness) address the electro*negativity* and aids in oxygenating the neshama (soul) and the world.

Here's a "heavy metal" element on the periodic table of life, "The only person you should try to be better than is the person you were yesterday."

Please keep in mind, the past is in your head. The future is in your hands.

Keep the HP (Higher Power) perspective." It's been said, "A sharp mind will find a truth for itself. A humble spirit will find a truth higher than itself. Truth is not the property of intellectuals, but of those who know how to escape their own selves."

What we are is what we're not. Ultimately, "Our souls are not hungry for fame, comfort, wealth, or power. Our souls are hungry for meaning."

32

UniverseSoully Yours

Dear sentient being,

"They that love beyond the world cannot be separated by it. Death cannot kill what never dies. Nor can spirits ever be divided that love & live in that same Divine principle."

Some say, "You only live once. No, you may die once, but you live everyday."

C.S. Lewis said, "If the whole universe has no meaning, we should never have found out that it has no meaning: just as, if there were no light in the universe and therefore no creatures with eyes, we should never know it was dark. Dark would be without meaning." The universe not only has physical meaning, it also has spiritual meaning.

The Zohar provides us with a deep appreciation of life beyond life; of secrets that stretch beyond the naked eye of this world, believe not that man consists solely of flesh, skin, bones, and veins. The real part of man is his soul, and the things just mentioned, the skin, flesh, bones, and veins, are only an outward covering, a veil, but are not the man. When man departs he divests himself of all the veils which cover him. And these different parts of our body correspond to the secrets of the Divine wisdom. The skin typifies the heavens which extend everywhere and cover everything like a garment. The flesh puts us in mind of the darker side of the universe. The bones and the veins symbolize the Divine chariot, the inner powers of man which are the servants of G-d. But they are all but an outer covering. For, inside man, there is the secret of the Heavenly Man… Everything below takes place in the same manner as everything above. This is the meaning of the remark that G-d created man in His own image. But just as in the heavens, which cover the whole universe, we behold different shapes brought about by the stars and the planets to teach us concerning hidden things and deep secrets, so upon the skin which covers our body there are shapes and forms which are like planets and stars to our bodies. All these shapes have a hidden meaning.

Our being contains and is vivified by a spark of Infinity. A morsel of the Prime Mover, Hashem. We are all sourced in the Source of all sources. There's a deep-rooted connectivity among the physical, mental, celestial & spiritual anatomy which energizes all existence. Here one arrives at the intersection where the finite meets the Infinite. It's this cultivated relationship that helps each of us transcend and elevate this lower level world ever higher.

Each individual stands at various crossroads throughout the duration of this life. Shed preconceived notions. Remain reachable, teachable, universal. The One universe-soul is calling, guiding and showing us the path through the darkness and light of each of our lives.

Rabbi Ashlag offered, "There is one unified soul. In it, all of our souls are linked closely together. They are bonded with the force of Love, the only law that exists... The Creator broke this one unified soul, and now we have to restore that union by ourselves. That is, we have to rise above our egos, up to the degree of Love."

Rav Kook expressed, "The Second Temple was destroyed because of causeless hatred. Perhaps the Third will be rebuilt because of causeless love." He also shared, when we find the kernel of good inside the depths of evil and grasp it, polish it, and expand it, and find that which must be taken from it and put into practice, this is how the sparks rise to their holy place.

Elevating these sparks is a process of salvaging the good, positive, light, and uncovering the worthiness and contribution every experience. It's is a process of extricating the sparks from the outer shells (klipos) that envelope them and fulfilling the hidden divine potential that yearns to be revealed and realized.

A mystic divulged, the universe is one. Everything and everyone is interconnected through an invisible web of stories. Whether we are aware of it or not, we are all in a silent conversation. Do no harm. Practice compassion. And do not gossip behind anyone's back – not even a seemingly innocent remark! One man's pain, hurts us all. One man's joy, will make everyone smile.

Hashem is the Eternal One. Our souls are a piece of eternity, truly death defying. Let's open our eyes to the infinite spirit that moves through all things. It's universal. Settle up; for the soul of the matter is a matter of the soul.

A scientist once indicated, "There's as many atoms in a single molecule of your DNA as there are stars in the typical galaxy. We are, each of us, a little universe."

Each one of us is a universal, eternal soul carrying about a temporary body.

What's perceived as "demise" can't kill what does not die. The eternality of the soul beckons to the Infinite. For, "I am Yours. Don't give myself back to me."

Time is the pulse of the universe. Everything is right on time and in its place. Divine inscriptions are everywhere. We shall not be separated from these undying insignias if we love and live with divine principles. It's signed on nature and inscribed in space and time. Connect the dots. See the signals and sign on the dotted lifeline. A universal *sign*ature for all humankind.

UnivereSoully yours throughout all time.

33

Abracadabra

Poof!

It appears investigation on the word has unearthed its origin in the Aramaic/Hebrew vernacular, in which *abra* means "to create" and *cadabra* which means "as I say", offering an adaptation of abracadabra as "create as I say" or "with my words I create." Words can create. Words breathe and animate. Words can deflate or words can levitate and resuscitate.

In this high-tech, fast paced- sleight of hand world- words are so often used flippantly; almost without contemplation or awareness. Stringing together sentences without prudence has become commonplace. Presto! Loshon hara materializes from out of thin air. Chicanery and illusion are brought into being as frequent as the proverbial rabbit being pulled out of a hat. It's a 24/7 magic (tragic) show with nothing to show for it but mumbo-jumbo and defamation. Smoke and mirrors are not needed to distinguish with lucidity the damaging or healing, spellbinding power of words. Make sure to cast the right "spell" on words or it could have the wrong effect/affect on the audience and the recipient(s). Wait the shows not over...

Perplexingly, many only see the optics and not what's behind the curtains.

In this week's parsha – Balak: speech and words play an integral role. It was not by vaporous mist, legerdemain or incantation that speech/words created. Balak speaks to Bilaam and employs him to curse the Jews. Bilaam's donkey miraculously makes use of words; however it falls on deaf ears. Bilaam's malignant scheme was to unleash venomous curses upon the Jews, but G-d shifted Bilaam's intended curses into a potpourri of blessings! Behold. Abracadabra! Blessings crystallized from proposed maledictions.

Don't be an illusionist. Be an illuminant. Bring light into the words you release internally (within yourself) and externally (with others). Construct speech that will, "pull a rabbit out of a hat" so to speak, and reveal unity & opportunity.

Mystically speaking, "The words that come out of our mouths do not vanish but are perpetually stored in infinite space and they will come back to us in due time."

The Baal ShemTov expressed, with every word and expression that leaves your lips, have in mind to bring about a Unification.

Words create on all levels and dimensions; no wand required. It's no trick that G-d will unremittingly shield Israel from the magicians (archaic or contemporary). The hand (of G-d) is quicker than the eye (of man). No subterfuge. No vanishing acts. No hocus-pocus... Hashem's word will never disappear.

34

+ ÷ × −

For the sake of discussion let's suppose the presented mathematical symbols are a paradigm of the human condition and life cycle. Add + = we are born. Divide ÷ = we divide into our respective factions, groups, partners (spouse and family) or being riddled with a degree of indecision. Multiply × = we multiply, pro-create or use our creativity/ingenuity to expand. Subtract − = we pass away. If only the process (life & death) could be broken down in such rudimentary terms. Nevertheless, each of us inhabits in or between the aforementioned. Seems trivial? Take pause and in the silence regain composure. Life is far more than flesh and blood, oxygen and carbon dioxide, atoms and molecules, black holes and string theory. Simple, yet so meticulously layered with complexity.

Math as it is affords us the ability to crunch the numbers and leaves no room for mistakes; it has been labeled the perfect science and a universal language. So what drives these symbols and its numbers? The human calculator?

Math supposedly doesn't lie, but we do.

Since time immemorial humankind has grappled with the question, "what is the meaning of life?" Nowadays many are waxing philosophical. Where does such an answer(s) reside? Does math contain the answer(s)? Much postulation has given rise to even more speculation. Indubitably it cannot measure the worth of a person. The value of each individual is intrinsic- not extrinsic. Not based on stats and numbers in the final analysis. However, it is based on a resolute moral fortitude.

It's not what's the meaning of life, but rather what gives life meaning? By answering the latter the former can be solved. A most existentially spiritual equation calculates, answers, and then dispels the most perplexing of axioms, theorems, proofs by reasoning's—inferencing— trivial proof, vacuous proof, proof by contrapositive and proof by contradiction. With this angle problem solving is presented in a more spiritually visceral and cerebral perspective which is equivalent to your uniqueness. As the Baal Shem Tov said, "Everybody is unique. Compare not yourself with anybody else lest you spoil G-d's curriculum." People ask, "where is G-d?" G-d doesn't move. People move (in mindset and perspective). So the real question is, "where are you?" What equation are you living in? You are the individual quotient, as you are a non-repeating decimal. Get the point? There is only one you and there is only One G-d. That equals to two too and two is indicative of a relationship.

On the other side of the equation, the world is replete with the Korach attitude. This is patently obvious in those trying to discredit G-d, the Torah's authenticity and its leadership. Dismantling and disconnecting from the spiritual equation through various modes of intellectualization, emotions and a cornucopia of defense mechanisms. Each having their own convoluted motivations or excuses for resenting and challenging the legitimacy of the Sinaitic experience. The Truth cannot truly be calculated, nor can it be measured. But it can be studied, inculcated and integrated into the variables, components and geometrics in life. By learning about and connecting to the Truth, we are earning! And in return, that is what gives life meaning and assists in solving life's problems. This is what really counts!

In conclusion, it's what we do in between the addition (birth) and subtraction (death) symbols that defines us in this formula and in due course determines our stats (mitzvos) when we are subtracted and depart from this arithmetical equation of a world called life. It's an ethereal equation of sublimity that stretches well beyond math and its symbols.

Go figure.

Add it up.

35

Clandestiny

A Jew's operation may seem clandestine to the naked eye. The Jew seeks to formulate a faithful home amid a world of contradictions and cacophony. A Jew in this vein makes no pomp and circumstance about his life but lives quietly in a spiritual manner which imposes upon none. This small and secret operation is on a covert level very few have comprehended.

The 19th century author Mark Twain has been noted for promulgating: "If the statistics are right, the Jews constitute but one percent of the human race. It suggests a nebulous dim puff of stardust lost in the blaze of the Milky Way. Properly the Jew ought hardly to be heard of, but he is heard of, has always been heard of. He is as prominent on the planet as any other people, and his commercial importance is extravagantly out of proportion to the smallness of his bulk. His contributions to the world's list of great names in literature, science, art, music, finance, medicine, and abstruse learning are also way out of proportion to the weakness of his numbers. He has made a marvelous fight in the world, in all the ages; and has done it with his hands tied behind him. He could be vain of himself, and be excused for it. The Egyptian, the Babylonian, and the Persian rose, filled the planet with sound and splendor, then faded to dream-stuff and passed away; the Greek and the Roman followed, and made a vast noise, and they are gone; other peoples have sprung up and held their torch high for a time, but it burned out, and they sit in twilight now, or have vanished. The Jew saw them all, beat them all, and is now what he always was, exhibiting no decadence, no infirmities of age, no weakening of his parts, no slowing of his energies and no dulling of his alert and aggressive mind. All things are mortal but the Jew; all other forces pass, but he remains. What is the secret of his immortality?"

The question posed by Mr. Twain has an answer. The true and authentic secret of the Jews immortality is Hashem, His Torah, Mitzvos and the sacred soul rooted in each Jew. This is not an elitist or discriminatory stance. This is not an egocentric movement. This is the centrality of the Jew. This is the destiny of this particular clan (The Jewish People). Mr. Twain made contact with the surface of the Jews immortality.

Shelach opens with the dispatching of the spies (a clandestine operation) to survey the land prior to entering Israel. The unsettling report the spies dispensed upon return sent shockwaves of fear which caused them to lose faith in the land which was divinely ordained for them. Consequently their entrance into Israel was deferred for well over three decades.

In contemporary times we are able to spy out our landscape with the compass of the Torah as our directional. Longitude, latitude, altitude and attitude all play a role in mapping the routes of our lives. Hashem provides the breeze, but we must raise the sails.

Rav Avigdor Miller stated, "a person may be burdened with many obstacles or handicaps that he was destined to have. That is his mazel, but he is able to utilize his freewill in a way to change his fate. And that which was meant as a detriment he can transform into a positive, allowing him to achieve greatness surpassing all those around."

The Jews clan destiny is clandestine to many. But it's no secret that the quiet whispers of holiness infused in an authentic Jewish life has the power to tame the roars of a feral world. Our faith begets our fate. This is our destiny as Jews. This is our *clan*destiny; a soft, unassuming transcendence from this world to the next.

36

Beyond Voyage

As we traverse the outer limits of the Solar System, we are faced with a vast emptiness. Beyond our home system lies the great mysteries of deep space. Here, the distances are so great as to boggle the mind. We can only look out into that emptiness with our telescopes and be humbled at the wonder of it all.

Enter G-d: the Creator and Author of all existence. If we are humbled by the wonder of it all through our telescopic projections, we should be all the more so awestruck and humbled by it all in relation to G-d!

Albert Einstein said, "Everyone who is seriously involved in the pursuit of science becomes convinced that a spirit is manifest in the laws of the universe. A spirit vastly superior to that of man, and one in the face of which we with our modest powers must feel humble. He added, "We are in the position of a little child entering a huge library filled with books in many different languages. The child knows someone must have written those books. It does not know how. It does not understand the languages in which they are written. The child dimly suspects a mysterious order in the arrangement of the books but doesn't know what it is. That seems to me, is the attitude of even the most intelligent being toward G-d. We see a universe marvelously arranged and obeying certain laws, but only dimly understand those laws. Our limited minds cannot grasp the mysterious force that moves the constellations."

Astronaut E Mitchell noted, "When I went to the moon I was a pragmatic test pilot. But when I saw the planet Earth floating in the vastness of space the presence of Divinity became almost palpable and I knew that life in the universe was not just an accident."

In a sense, we are all astronauts, space-walkers, space-travelers, soulnauts, travelling through space and time in attempt to dock at the Fathership (G-d). This is our main mission. Passing through all the space debris and galactic pollution to connect with the Infinite. Using the limits of time & space to transcend time and space. This is deep space in its deepest sense. Beyond any boundary or measure. Beyond human. Beyond beyond.

Good luck, G-dspeed, and bon voyage (beyond voyage) on this journey to Infinity, on this voyage beyond!

37

Out from Within

Did Pesach really work? Meaning, did we come out of the personal inner/outer Mitzrayim?

If we tried/try to integrate the deep messages of Passover sincerely then we should be perpetually endeavoring to emancipate ourselves (w/ the help of Hashem) from the very things that have held/hold us incarcerated on so many levels. Or are we back to "life as usual"; doing, saying & acting as if we just paid lip service to the whole thing. Simply "going through the motions" as if we just passed-over Passover & consequently missed the personal messages and the tikkunim (rectifications) of Pesach.

When and how will we make the sustainable changes many of us yearn for? When will we truly come closer to Hashem in action, speech and thought?

Jewish mystics discuss humanity being made in the image of G-d as an ongoing creative linkage to G-d's divine attributes (Sefiros) as a sacred tool for humankind's refinement & development. The Sefiros are ten channels or modalities through which Hashem conducts the universe. Being made in Hashem's image through Kabbalistic lenses means we have the power emulate Him via the attributes/emanations, the Sefiros.

Rabbi Avinoam Fraenkel presents a penetrating teaching from Reb Chaim Volozhin in that, "a Jew is a hybrid being containing components from all the world levels and a Jews deeds actively create, maintain & influences in some capacity all of the world levels." Using the Sefiros can help facilitate the aforementioned and moderate a positive influence and awakening from above which engenders an awakening from below & vice versa.

Tapping into the spiritual properties by counting the Omer is mitzvah that connects Pesach to Shavuos and us to Hashem. It's a time for active personal growth in which we are afforded the opportunity to use the seven week period as a refinery to cleanse & balance ourselves in preparation for receiving the eternal gift, the Torah. Each of the seven weeks correspond to one of the lower seven Sefiros. The first week & sefirah is Chesed kindness. The second week/sefirah is Gevurah strength/restraint. The third week/sefirah is Tiferes beauty. The fourth week/sefirah is Netzach victory. The fifth week/sefirah is Hod submission/thanks. The sixth week/sefirah is Yesod foundation. The seventh week/sefirah is Malchus kingdom. Synergistically these emanations culminate at Shavuos.

Take the inner journey to make Pesach count by utilizing

Sefiros HaOmer and engage in a personal tikun (reparation) of one's nature and the negative character traits within ourselves. In this capacity we make Pesach (& thereafter) effectively work & indubitably count by coming out (of Mitzrayim) from within (ourselves) when it really counts.

38

NASA (Need Another Spiritual Antidote)

...This is Mission Control...Are you ready?... You are wherever your thoughts are. Make sure your thoughts are where you want to be (Likutey Moharan 1:21). Thoughts are perpetually orbiting the sphere of the mind. As long as a person lives, thoughts exist. Some thoughts demand decisions. In the constellation of contemplation humans are blessed with the opportunity to make decisions. Some decisions are constructive, creating new worlds and potentiality, while others are more destructive, unleashing malefic black holes. At the origin of every decision is the metaphorical fork in the road. Choices. The commitment to a particular choice then spawns an outcome which in turn gives birth to fresh new thoughts and subsequently more decisions. The cyclical pattern repeats. In the womb of time thoughts are sheer abstractions until animated with the dynamics of pro-activity and actualization. All these ingredients- its variables and components have lit a course to this very "time and space" station in life.

"Space" food for thought: "I think therefore I am." I think not. "I am therefore I think." Because you have been given life which is sponsored by G-d and supplied with a moral compass (Torah) you are sustained (live) and are imbued with the capacity to think. The lifescape is infused with a myriad of thoughts which traffic between heaven and earth. With the Torah you are able utilize your thoughts to make appropriate decisions which manufacture salubrious outcomes both in the physical and spiritual world(s).The Torah acts as a spiritual orbital plane and a true axis between spirit and matter, physical and metaphysical. Living with the Torah in this space age we are permitted to gracefully age both in amplitude and altitude.

In Sichos Haran 46 it is revealed that the higher the faculty, the further it can reach. You can kick something with your foot but typically can throw something higher with your hand. Voice can reach even further as in calling someone from a distance. Audible range stretches yet further, because you can hear sounds like gunfire from a great distance. While vision reaches even further still, as you can see the sun, moon, stars, certain celestial bodies etc...The highest of all is the mind with which one can ascend the loftiest of heights. Thoughts in one's mind are truly among G-d's wonders. It is therefore paramount to endeavor to guard the mind and thoughts.

The part of the brain that gives you the ability to think is called the prefrontal cortex, which carries out executive functions. These functions are what makes the human brain so specialized, and distinguishes you from the rest of creation. By means of employing your thoughts to distill and pilot your emotions you can maximize your human potential. Furthermore when you occupy your mind with thoughts of Torah and devotion, all chambers of your heart will be on full throttle for G-d. Spiritual yearning and purity will eradicate the worldly pollution. By peeling away the stratums of atmospheric toxins one is able to unearth the astronomical power of thought. The nebulous becomes lucid and the ability to bring new vitality into one's mind invigorates the soul.

As terrestrial beings we are all "spacecraft"; as we occupy "space" on this earth and we must attempt to "craft" our thoughts and lives accordingly. As Jews we "shall be as numerous as the stars in the sky"- a most noteworthy star-cluster in the cosmos. And though the onerous gravitational pull of life/work on this planet may be palpable; NASA (Need Another Spiritual Antidote) is available for contact on a regular basis for spiritual fuel and amelioration. Embeded in the control pannel is the polychromatic flashing lights of: Shabbos, Yom Tov, Mitzvos, Torah, Tefilah and more; all available at our fingertips as Jews.

We're taking it way back before the so called Big Bang; to that holy, scared "place" and Energy that permeates all space and time. Infinite Light years prior to existence and reality as we know it.

The mission is mapped to bring universal awareness of the Infinite One. Thoughts unified and aligned; we are poised for interstellar mobility, the luminescent trajectory. We are catalyzing the launch. Commencing, the countdown is on...5...4...3...2...1...

Liftoff!

39

The Prism of the Mind

A prism refracts light. White light is composed of many different frequencies and wavelengths; a different frequency will correspond to a different color of light. When the light travels through the prism, it slows the light down and will refract it. Each frequency that makes up the white light slows down differently from each other, and thus refract at different angles and hence the presentation of seven colors arranged in order of decreasing wavelengths.

Behalosecha opens with a description of how to light the seven lamps of the Menorah. Rashi connotes that the word Behalosecha (when you light) literally means, "when you raise up." When one kindles a flame, it rises up.

Rabbi Chaim Kramer set us ablaze with the fires from Rebbe Nachman's magnum opus Likutey Moharan and illuminates, "The Menorah has seven lamps, or candles. A person's head corresponds to the Menorah: his "seven candles" are his two eyes, two ears, two nostrils and his mouth. When he sanctifies his "seven candles" –sanctifying his mouth by refraining from speaking falsehood, his nose by inculcating the awe of G-d, his ears by listening and having faith in the sages and his eyes by shutting them against evil– then the flame of his heart will rise and illumine his face with a G-dly light" (Likutey Moharan I,21).

From here on Earth, from our perspective, each of us is engaged in a personal battle to get to Olam Haba. We experience life through the seven aforementioned lamps or lights. We absorb and translate life through the prism of our minds, the brain. Just as a prism refracts light, so too our minds in a sense are like a prism refracting the light (or lack thereof) of our circumstance(s); which then in turn, colors our frame of mind. This is how we experience life both sensory and perceptually.

It's been said, "We bring light into this world not as a source but as a prism – it comes through us. As electricity requires a conduit, so spirit moves through human beings to touch others in crucial moments."

Rabbi Ginsburgh indicated, the Ba'al Shem Tov taught that the numerical value of the word for 'light' in Hebrew – 'ohr' – is 207, identical to the Hebrew word for 'secret' – 'raz'. He explained that when a person knows the raz/secret of another individual, he can shine his light upon him. Befittingly, the number 207 is also the numerical value of Ain Sof, 'Infinity'. The secret in the heart of every person is the infinite, as yet unfulfilled potential concealed within him. The light rectifies our eyes so that we can see this concealed secret in others, illuminate them, open their eyes to their infinite potential and guide them to make good use of their strengths.

The commonality linking the seven lamps spoken of and the prism of the mind is the number seven. The seven lights/lamps could also be correlated to the seven colors in the color-light spectrum: red, orange, yellow, green, blue, indigo and violet; this is the span of continuous spectrum of colors. The distinct bands are an artifact of human color vision also known as the acronym Roy G. Biv. This is how we see and experience things in our world (Olam Hazeh) through frequencies and wavelengths. If we keep the seven lamps polished it will allow for the pure light of G-d to shine through the prism of our minds and souls; then our world will be properly refracted and casted in an arrray of colors spiritually, mentally and physically. However, if we invoke the yetzer hara, the lamps become tarnished and the prism becomes obscured, thereby tainting the light and diminishing the colors in our life.

In lighting the lamps of our lives let's avoid striking and stoking the capricious flames that fuel a living inferno. Rather, let's use our "seven lamps" and the prism of our mind(s) refractions as tinder to ignite holy sparks that will generate beautiful flames. Sparking a spiritual conflagration that will rise up and set our hearts and souls on fire for Hashem! For as it states in Proverbs 20:27, "the soul of man is the lamp of G-d."

40

3D in Forty

To be in 3D is explained and projected as, "a three-dimensional model that displays a picture or item in a form that appears to be physically present with a designated structure. Principally, it allows items that appeared flat to the human eye to be displayed in a form that permits for various dimensions to be characterized. These dimensions embrace width, depth, and height."

In this week's parsha Ki Sisa Moshe ascends Sinai for 40 days and nights. When Moshe does not return when anticipated from Mount Sinai, impatience and disbelief takes root and the people sculpt a golden calf and worship it. G-d proposes to abolish the errant nation, but Moshe intercedes on their behalf. Moshe descends from the mountain carrying the tablets of the testimony emblazoned with the Ten Commandments; seeing the people with the idol, he shatters the tablets and destroys the golden calf.

Subsequently, Moshe prepares a new set of tablets on the

mountain for 40 more days and nights, where G-d reinscribes the indenture on these second tablets. On the mountain, Moses is also granted a vision of the divine thirteen attributes of mercy which is the prescription for teshuvah. G-d forgives the people for their flagrancy in worshiping the idol.

Perceptually and virtually life is casted and experienced in 3D in numerous ways, shapes and angles. On this plane the vertical and the horizontal don't always coalesce. Many of us struggle to merge the horizontal (living here on earth and our desires) and the vertical (spiritual aspirations and relationship with G-d). Often a malaise sets in. The perils of living in 3D become ever-present. The corrosive elements of melancholy roll in and paint the perceptions with the darkest tones and textures. In some cases, tablets are dispensed in order to address the intrusive and most salient symptoms.

There are two tablets (luchos) dispensed by G-d and brought down by Moshe from Sinai that we can ingest for our mental, physical and spiritual health; a time-release capsule and prescription that also aids in quelling the paroxysms of anxiety and downheartedness. The result is a life lived in horizontal and vertical harmony and stabilization. The forty days and nights that Moshe spent to bring down and dispense the new tablets were meant to brighten and enliven our experience being animated by 3D in forty(4D) (4-Directions-North, South, East and West). In Kabbalah, forty is representative of the four directions which each direction contains ten Sefirot. Forty in Jewish literature also is related to transformation and renewal.

These sacred tablets given to Moshe by G-d are for us to take and use as prescribed. The Torah is the script for the body, mind and soul. Added to your regular regimen these tablets are meant to be taken per diem and have been proven in trials (& tribulations) to effect change and add vigor to the three dimensions of mental, physical and spiritual well being. The result is a truly pervasive 3D effect to life that you can see and feel.

41

Enlightening Bolts

The jagged symmetry of life intermittently lights pathways and spells out circumstances we had not necessarily forecasted in our personal sky dome. This atmospheric discharge of electricity can potentially electrocute circuitry- causing a seeming loss of power.

However, within the auspicious time frame between Pesach and Shavuos we have a unique opportunity to shape these so-called bolts by counting Sefirah. The Torah commands us to count forty-nine days from the second day of Pesach to Shavuos. Taking the number 49 and adding up the separate digits 4 and 9 equals 13. Thirteen is the gematria (numerical equivalent) of echad (one) and ahava (love). Counting is ascension in this case, as we count up and draw closer to G-d's Oneness while simultaneously sparking G-d's infinite love for us and our love for G-d.

When we departed Egypt, we had descended to the 49th level of tumah, spiritual degradation. By counting each day, we mount one step higher, catapulting to new altitudes in spirituality and holiness. During Sefiras HaOmer we have the inimitable possibility to conduct spiritual electricity. The electricity can be honed at this juncture, as we strive to develop and fine tune ourselves for the apex; the transmission and receiving of the Torah on Shavuos. Each day is infused with its own high voltage (or voltage from on High) which permits us to recharge our relationship with G-d and each other by working on our character traits. It is the electrical field and the spectrum of the human experience that flows within the power lines of each day. A direct feed from the Infinite power station to us.

Just as we have the Counting of the Omer to produce consecrated bolts, we must also have the means to continue to generate inspiration. Rabbi Akiva Tatz explains, "The Rambam depicts life as a dark ominous night on a stormy plain – lashed by the rain, misplaced in the darkness, one is faced with desolation. Suddenly, there is a flash of lightning! In a millisecond the landscape is as clear as day, one's direction is observable. But just as soon as it is perceived it disappears and one must fight on through the tempest with only the recollection of that flash for guidance. The lightning (inspiration) lasts very briefly…How can we cull this bursting surge of energy and emotion and convert it into additional enlightening bolts of inspiration?" He continues and shares from the Zohar, "through the darkness of ordeals, the light of personal growth is revealed."

What sort of lightning rod is required to conduct this sort

of spiritually inspired electricity? The earthly (and celestial) grid is lit up by the mega-volts streaming and contained in Torah, tefillah and mitzvos! The bolts are formed from air to ground and ground to air- for it is an electrifying life-giving current that potentially strikes and passes through each of us. "As lightning springs out of its concealment in dark clouds to flash through the world, so the divine light, embedded in matter, emerges through charitable deeds…Thus, through charity, a sort of divine revelation occurs in the soul," shared the Baal HaTanya. Hashem is charitable to us. We should strive to conduct ourselves with magnanimity.

Blessed and strengthened we stand primed to weather many a storm. Static cling to G-d and Torah and we will attract our own personal lightning bolts – bolts of enlightenment that flash and pierce the darkness so we can see the path.

Relationships are like electric currents. Wrong connection(s) will give you shocks throughout your life, but the right ones will light up your life.

Conduct and craft your own bolts, volts and jolts of inspiration to empower and light up your life and the lives of others. Get struck by enlightening bolts!

You may find this rather shocking, but the One and only divine electric company has been supplying the power from the beginning.

42

It's Not Them

The plagues are introduced in this week's parsha, Va'eira. The plagues cascade and strike upon Pharaoh and the Egyptians. However, Rav Avigdor Miller shares a thought on the makos (plagues). Rav Miller conveyed that the plagues were not for Pharaoh and the Egyptians. G-d could have afflicted Pharaoh with some deathly or grave illness that would have called for his demise. Rav Miller divulged, "the makos were not for the Egyptians, they were for us, the Jews;" "in order that you should know." Rav Miller extended that not only the plagues spelled out in the Torah, but all makos we go through are for us to know(G-d).

A common response to problems that arise is to seek out a formula to blame others or shift the responsibility from ourselves. This attitudinal approach sets a most unsettling tone and has a propensity to cripple self-growth. To totally blame someone or something for all ailments and troubles that befall one is a lame excuse. Blame causes the blamer to "b"lame.

The truth is everything that happens to us both personally and nationally is "for us to know." There is a lesson in each maka (affliction) in life. It is for us; it is not about the other person or people. It's not them.

Gleaning the lesson from Rav Miller we see clearly that G-d is in total control. This is the message linked and harnessed to the plagues; knowing that this is G-d's world. This takes a lifetime of work and continuous inculcation.

Stubbornness is poured and settles on the heart like concrete; just like Pharaoh who initially refused to see G-d in the plagues. "A hardened heart." In many ways we encounter that personal Pharaoh within ourselves. Rejecting the makos in our lives. Revolting against the afflictions and declining to see G-d in the details. Here again, here we stand, right back in the arid winds of Egypt with a dry mouth and mind. Not allowing us to be freed from the slavish ways of the world and the cult of personality.

"Let my people go" starts with each one of us individualistically. Let me go. Let the "I" go; brush the sands of Egypt from the eyes (I's). It's not them. The makos are for each of us (to know G-d). It's not them. It's us and Hashem!

43

Souldier

Atten Hut!

Throughout time the battle fields have changed but the prize has always remained the same: the human soul.

There is an internal battle incessantly raging. A war machine churning and it has its sights set on swaths of land and the immeasurable territory of the soul. The fight of all time is between the yetzer hara (negative inclination) and the yetzer tov (positive inclination). This melee extends outside the borders of the standard war theater.

Rabbi Freeman implores us, "Look deeply within each person you encounter, no matter how brilliant or dull, refined or crude, righteous or wicked you judge this person to be. Beyond their clothes, beyond their skin, beyond their behavior, beyond their words. Beyond the emotions they show, the personality in which they dress, past whatever masks they don to conceal their inner woes. Look deeply and see the vicious war each one fights inside, the battle to remain human in a maddening world—a world you will never know, for no two of us are placed in the same world and no two of us confront the same challenges—the sickness at knowing one's own failures and deficiencies, the yearning to be more, the disappointment at not being that, the struggle to fight every sorrow, every pain, every plummeting, disastrous trauma of life...True, perhaps not everyone fights every battle. Some have long surrendered.But the very fact that this person was assigned this battle tells us more than can be spoken, for the One who created him knows he has the power to prevail and win. That alone is enough to admire, and to be humbled, asking yourself, "Do I fight a battle nearly as fierce as the one I expect this person to win? In what way am I any better?" Be an denizen of the soul.

Sometimes the enemy is in-a-me. The yetzer hara is an inside terrorist lurking, sitting, waiting to ambush a souldier. Cunning and deleterious is this radical inclination that uses all sorts of camouflages and biological, chemical and psychological warfare. A souldier must stand in readiness to combat this rancorous beast and deactivate any traps or land mines. To be stalwart and unrelenting in this conflict is to overthrow the arsenal of insidious strategies that may confuse and take a souldier off his course.

If taken as a POW or in no man's land a souldier must do an about face and turn his course using his compass, with the directional instrument of teshuvah and Torah he may surely find his direction again. No ceasefires can be called against such an adversary unless one can take his yetzer hara captive and brainwash it to and for the good. Only then can one stake claim to a victorious counteroffensive.

Never go AWOL or abort a good mission consisting of prayer, repentance and charity. As Jews we must be valiant! Taking dawn and night patrol in vigilance against sneak attacks. A souldier must fortify himself and deploy all tactics to neutralize the lethality of yetzer hara. Dispatch all vessels; air, land and sea.

A souldier is demanded to have a plan/counterattack and it is his duty be on a reconnaissance mission, scouting out territorial surroundings in thought and deed. While simultaneously avoiding zones of fire, artillery barrage, bullets, blitzkriegs, breaches and assaults from all angles and on all senses. So know, in the war of the ego, the loser always wins.

Respect a souldier as one stands as vanguard of faith. Don't go MIA (missing in action) when the One and Only the Commander in Chief calls to you! Put your boots on the ground, lock & load, and put MIA (mitzvos in action). Answer to the chain of command. Fight the night with faith and light.

Rank and file as we are roll called to the highest order in G-ds battalion of the utmost caliber. The Citadel nation as such is the Jewish nation. A bastion of spiritual valor is each souldier in this infantry. A Jew is a member of a spiritual brigade and armament of faith and trust. Service awards are stockpiled & earned as ribbons, medals and others honors for each and every enlisted souldier (via the performance of mitzvos). A ground and air offensive of mitzvos can weaken the yetzer hara's front and reinforce the yetzer tov. Spearheaded by this conquest via a life test.

Mili*torah*y intelligence affords tactical maneuvers through overt and clandestine operations of Torah, prayer and mitzvos (TPM) which provide the logistics. Don't go in far red rather initiate the night vision gear and the new-clear weapon (TPM) as profound heavenly, triumphant exit strategy.

Forward march! The is your Torah of duty. Onward souldier through the blockades, through the debris and shrapnel. Advance souldier for you are cut and hewn from the finest. Have a stouthearted, valorous faith to carry you through every fight. Keep your head up. Hashem gives the hardest battles to the strongest souldiers. You are a *soul*dier, one of the few, the proud, the Jew. No retreat, as the battle cry echoes throughout the chambers of your soul! A salute to one nation under One G-d.

44

Haunted Words (Grave Chatter)

A word is defined as, "a unit of language, consisting of one or more spoken sounds or their written representation that functions as a principal carrier of meaning. Words are composed of one or more morphemes and are either the smallest units susceptible of independent use or consist of two or three such units combined under certain linking conditions."

A word unaccompanied can transmit meaning. Words linked together communicate concepts and emotions which have the propensity to summon a response and impel action. Civilizations and cultures have been born with words. Civilizations and cultures have been disseminated or destroyed with words that have grave consequences. Words live well beyond the duration or average lifespan of a human. Words have the power to conjure and conquer. Furthermore, "a meaningful silence is always better than meaningless words."

Ghosts are explained to be supernatural. Words themselves have a spirit and are supernatural, having the power to haunt and preoccupy. Words can arouse specters of the past or form phantoms of present. Words have a presence, at times not seen, but unquestionably heard, sensed and felt. Our minds become haunted house(s) as the words float and reside as a memory or materialize as images that occupy our mind, thoughts and emotions. Words have an ethereal affect and effect. Words have the uncanny ability to be wraithlike, vampiric and hurt or words can have an aura of healing; all the while nevertheless, haunting many habitats and atmospheres. Words make an impression on the living. Words are double edged as evidence by rearranging the word "words" which reveals the word "sword." Words can injure and damage like a sword or build and protect like a sword. For it has been said, "the pen is mightier than the sword."

The parsha of Mattos invokes vows and oaths. Words spoken (or written) in a promissory manner are to be actualized and if the words transporting the promise are not "brought to life" then lashes are imposed. To "give your word" carries weight and has a paranormal life of its own. It is transparent and apparent that the apparitional influence of words is a force (that beckons). The Torah conveys that our words are binding. The Torah's words live everlastingly. Our words of Torah are undying, enduring and protect us, thus bridging the world of the living and departed.

As we draw near Chumash Devarim (words) and Tisha B'Av lets us recall the grave, haunting memories of the Beis

Hamikdash being destroyed because of groundless hatred and loshan hara (negative/damaging speech) . A "say"ance should be performed. What is said (or written) has the power to take life or raise the dead (so to speak). Words are ghostly, vaporous and phantastic. Words can decompose or compose the lives it passes through. Words linger and carry a living "die"lect which are strung up and held together by a poltergeist of sentence structure. A passing word and sentence can sentence and incarcerate for years or emancipate and liberate one from the bondage of such ghastly verbiage. A word slinger uses the atmosphere as a canvas and has a choice to paint it with fear and negativity or cheer and positivity. The disembodied quality of words can be seen moving objects(tives) in life in one way or another. Each life as such is a phenomenal "ghost" story of sorts. Let's be compelled to dispel the ignis fatuus.

In a mystical sense, "the words you speak become the house you dwell in." Is your residency haunted? Is this the haunted how's we allow ourselves to take residence in? Are we mere denizens of this area drifting among the ghost prattle? Often, the haunted house is in our head.

The Chofetz Chaim said, "For every moment that a person closes his mouth [and refrains from speaking loshon hora] he merits a hidden light that no angel or earthly creature can fathom."

Something is in the air; a faint presence, a chill, a manifestation beseeching us, speaking to us to inspect our words and their impact if we want to have a "ghost of a chance." The in-visible force of words by no means give up the ghosts or die. There is no expiration date in this "grave"yard. No funeral. No RIP if words are used to bury others. If we're not cautious the tongue can also act as a shovel by digging our own grave. Words can bury or carry. Words don't rest; they often have a life of their own. They go on chattering beyond the grave, haunting for better or worse, long after each of us expires.

May we all learn to be vessels for speech that brings new hope, light & life to the world.

45

Tune into the Infinity Frequency

There's so much static and interference on this current station called LIFE 24.7. The fomenting dark waves, mega"hurts" and negative vibrations make for warped transmissions.

"Fortunately, some have spiritual immune systems that reject the illusory worldview grafted upon them through social conditioning. Instead of following the crowd they choose knowledge over the veils of ignorance," observed Jewish philosopher H. Bergson.

Terrestrial static can be fine tuned with an amplification of cosmic clarity. Thinking, speaking and acting in alignment with the Infinite metaphysically nourishes the world(s) according to the adroit Kabbalists.

Albert Einstein expressed beautifully, "We are slowed down sound and light waves, a walking bundle of frequencies tuned into the Cosmos. We are souls dressed up in sacred biochemical garments and our bodies are the instruments through which our souls play their music."

If you can't find a connection maybe it's because you can only see as far as you can think. Raise your standards, and Hashem will meet you there. The Torah provides the circuitry for improved awareness and frequency.

Understand, the right to choose your own path is a sacred privilege. Use it wisely.

Finding a clearer frequency is about seeking & maintaining a quality connection to truth, compassion, and not following the crowd. When trying to tune into life we often have to go through some static to find clear reception. It's about changing the channels to tune into the messages, data & appropriate units of shefa/flow of spiritual energy to receive a cleaner signal in sight, sound and outlook.

You are the embodiment of Divine light and frequency. Light emanated potentially multiplies light absorbed. Recognize your own origin. Align with the Cause of all causes. Enagaging the spiritual antennas enhances receptivity to tune into the Infinity frequency on High being immutably broadcasted from the omnipotent Emanator.

Transmit with wisdom, "How do you fine-tune the soul? You have three knobs: What you do, what you say and what you think. Adjust them carefully for static-clean reception." Scan, seek, and plug in. Tap into this frequency frequently for enahnced definition and clarity. This can be modulated by celestial broadband reach in the vicinity of divinity with Infinity. We could all use some fine tuning. As it's been aired, "You are here on earth to unearth who on earth you are."

Please stay tuned…Tuning up is about learning what to tune in and what to tune out.

~ *Extracted from the authors first book* The Infinity Frequency

46

Near Life Experience

Will the real you please stand up?

It is patent that Avram stood and in doing so became Avraham, for real. Avraham is the vanguard and paragon of Monotheism. The seedlings of Judaism were planted in his recognition that there is One G-d, One Prime Mover. Avraham deracinated himself from his environment and blazed a new path & life. Deserting the sights, sounds and smells he was accustomed to for higher and holier grounds.

Avraham exemplifies the soul of a person who wishes to align himself with G-d. Reb Noson of Breslov enlightens, "Such a person must depart from his "land" (materialism), his "birthplace" (his sensual pleasures & depression), and his "father's house" (family who attempts to persuade or stop him from serving G-d). Furthermore, by leaving behind your past and embracing spirituality, even though you may later descend to "Egypt"(the challenges and difficulties of life) you will have the intestinal fortitude to ascend from there and even take with you many sparks of holiness" (Likutey Halachos II. p. 145a).

Rabbi Moshe Alshich comments that the word "lecha" seems to be superfluous. For if Hashem was informing Avraham to "go" it could of simply said "Lech." The Alshich reveals that "Lech lecha" means more than just "go"; it's conveying – "go to yourself, go to your essence." Avraham understood this. When G-d spoke to Avraham and said "Lech lecha" these two words would set the tone for Jews to come and continues to reverberate to this very day. Judaism came to life on the breath of these words. The world came to life! The world was undergoing a NDE (Near Death Experience) until Avraham made a personal "Lech lecha" (lit."go to yourself" or "go for yourself"). Avraham ignited his & each Jewish soul with his trailblazing "Lech lecha." That very non-extinguishable flame burns on in each of us. There is a well known saying that, "every man dies but not every man really lives." Avraham resuscitated and inaugurated the world to the truest form of spirituality. He really lived!

Hear the eternal call, "Lech lecha." It's time to go. We must attempt to make on ongoing "Lech lecha" in our daily lives. We must go to our essence. That is to establish a life confirming link to the Essence of all essences. Whether FFB (Frum from birth) or BT (Baal teshuva) it is crucial for us to take a stand. For, "if you don't stand for something, you'll fall for anything." G-d is saying, "Lech lecha" to each of us right now; "go to yourself, go for yourself, go to your essence." Go to a deeper you. Go for the preservation and augmentation of your very life, your soul; as our forefather Avraham did. In doing so the real you will radiate, and in the process the authentic you will stand up.

Life is swarming with NDEs; by making your own "Lech lecha" a NDE (Near Death Experience) is converted into a NLE (Near Life Experience) as we move closer to G-d, the Giver of all life, the true essence of everything. Know, that this is about as near to a real living experience as we can get in this life and in this flesh. Rabbi S.R. Hirsch conveyed, "Every breath drawn by an individual who truly serves G-d will elicit a responsive chord from the universe around him." It stands to reason that experiencing the reviving essence of being near Hashem is more than life giving. It's definitely death defying!

47

Coat of Cosmic Color

A coat is a garment which covers the body from shoulder to waist, knee or foot. Coat in its verb form is to cover with a layer or coating (as in a coat of paint). Or it can take a historical or heraldry form of a family badge or crest (coat of arms).

Parsashas Vayeishev is *coat*ed with a layer of preferential treatment. Jacob expresses his love and gives his son Joseph a coat of many colors. Rebbe Nachman relates: the verse says, "He (Ya'akov) made him (Yosef) a coat of many colors" (Genesis 37:3). He continues, "The Zohar conveys that every physical item in this world is rooted in the spiritual light of Hashem which consists of many different colors. That Ya'akov gave Yosef such a coat represents that he imparted to him the wisdom of manipulating physicality through the infinite cosmic colors of Hashem's light. Possessing this knowledge, Yosef was able to fathom the inner stitching's of the universe which enabled him to explain and demonstrate to all people how Hashem can be found in every nuance of the material world."

Yosef represents Yesod (Foundation). The foundation of sanctity. Yosef's coat of many colors could be said to represent the many facets of humankind and the many challenges and inner conflicts that we experience. Yosef was able to cultivate the supernal colors symbolized by his coat and control his baser urges. He was a man of many dreams who overcame many obstacles. He was thrown into the pit of despair, but never lost faith. He was jailed, but never spiritually held captive. He was master of self-control despite suffering. He remained coated in G-d's providence. Yosef recognized there are divine threads woven into the very galactic fabric of existence.

As we move from our past to present and onward into the future it is key it carry and don the lessons from the coat of many colors. We have our coat of arms; cosmic colors laced into the tapestry of our heritage. Covered in a protective cosmic coating of G-d's love we can weather many a challenges, storms and climates. Rabbi Nefesh imparts, "It is important to know that each one of us has spiritual clothing, which is made with energy we create with our actions. If we act negatively, we create clothing that invites trouble and chaos. Positive actions create clothing that will protect us when we need it."

An inner and outer coating of divinity is a common thread throughout Torah and prayer. It's the earthly, symbolic embodiment and binding force to keep us protected and comforted throughout life's chilling events. As Hashem's chosen and favored we are eternally wrapped and faithfully coated in a chromatic coat of cosmic color like no other.

48

Vital Signs

It's the cardiac event of a lifetime! Suspended between the oscillating pendulum of life and death...From ER to OR Condition: Critical.

At the heart of every beat are the vital signs of life, which provide the following objective measures for a person: temperature, respiratory rate, heart beat (pulse), and blood pressure. When these values are not zero, they signify that a person is alive. Alive or just existing and what about structural defects? Choose life over existence.

There is a correlation between the medical (physical) and spiritual. The signs of life are determined by spiritual pulse and respiration. This requires a count of the proclivities of the inner chambers and valves of the heart, demanding a self-surgical procedure.

Intervention #1: The examination of self. The most difficult surgeries are those performed on ourselves. These operations are routinely executed without anesthesia. Careful introspections (incisions) are made in order to thwart the death spiral. Attention is given to what is passing through the spiritual atria and ventricles. A self-accounting. An obstruction or clot must be dealt with in a timely fashion. Coagulation and rupture can invoke dire scenarios, a ripple effect. A caveat; what passes through the heart must pass through the mind and soul, triggering a spiritual-cardio-cerebral episode.

The exigency for open heart surgery in this capacity is a lifelong surgical modus operandi. The tools of the trade are featured through Intervention #2: In order to sustain the vital signs of our life we must take notice of the vital *signs* in life. The conduction pathway that G-d communicates to us is via nature and events which are the signs meant to guide us through the benign and malignant encounters, thereby terminating the arrhythmia. This faith-filled form of oxygenation makes for uninterrupted flow and eupnea. It is mandatory that the heart be open for optimum circulation and integration, allowing for proper distribution and cardiovascular health.

Decompensation is modulated *soul*y by injection. Intervention #3: אמת Emes (Truth), which stands at the threshold of every contour and symptom in life is a three-tiered inoculation; Alef, Mem, Tav. Acute observation reveals, dissecting the Alef from Emes results in Mem-Tav, Mes (death). Empirical-spiritual research dictates Alef as the numerical equivalent of one brings to light that the One (G-d) is Emes and without Alef (One-G-d) there is Mes (death) which is symptomatically distal from Emes. Emes is a de*fib*rillator as it eliminates and dispels sheker (falsehood) thus repolarizing the heart of the matter and the heart of the spirit. Alef- Mem-Tav (Emes-Truth) is the triple bypass that resuscitates life and is the most proximal to G-d.

Now faithfully sutured with an insurant future, treasure what's in the chest, as it leads to a chest full of treasure. The glistening electro-kinetic heart sparks arrange and revitalize the interior and exterior. A lifetime stint with G-d and Emes supports a clean bill of health; while simultaneously reviving the glowing heart light that illuminates the tenebrous corridors and restarts life's natural pacemaker. Accompanying each heartbeat, internal and external nutrients are carried and nursed to every cell, atom and molecule. Heart failure to heart success, cardiac arrest – arrested. Diagnosed and treated.

Postoperative data demonstrates significant evidence that the malady has been quelled by heeding and reading the vital signs which indicate life – its intervals, its peaks and valleys. A comforting recovery. A new ventilation, pulsation and recuperation. Prognosis: Re*jew*venation.

49

Awakening the Ambiance

Sincere one, what troubles you? Lend an ear – O, one who
seeks. A quest of questions. Are you embittered? *W*hat
venom has entered your veins? How much more poison can
you *take*? Beleaguered senses under siege. Have you lost
something? Nothing took it from you witho*ut p*ermission.
What are you looking for? Something more, something
better than bitter. What's missing? Grasp, input becomes
outlook. Tears tear at the heart. Purloined from your point
of vie*w*. "What you seek is seeking you." O ye, of little faith
and cyclopean ego, where will you find the lost object? Is
th*at* the subject? Where are you loo*k*ing? Who are you
looking to? Is it not all inside of you? Dual, vestibule.
Double-edged atmosphere. "U"nify. What's out of sight
must b*e* sound in mind. Yo*u*'ve struggled far too long. Tired
one, caught in a *p*erpetual yawn. A*wake*! Don't "fall" back to
sleep. Cease looking outside. It's time to come home. Is your

equation not adding *up*? Consider subtracting to add, adding
to subtract. Guileless one, friend, faith *w*ill t*ak*e you where
no man can. O child, depart from childhood. Remov*e* the
taste from your mouth. Voiceless words. Sacred utterances.
Unpl*u*mbed depths. Stepless ste*p*s. Room-less rooms. Catch
the drift. Inertia as an adhesive. Gravity releases. Arcane
textures. Wind found in the Tree. Mind blown by a
mystical, celestial, cerebral breeze. Rarefied air. Return to the
eternal *w*omb. Propinquity. Unlocked; unclocked cosmic
moment(s), timeless embr*a*ce. Revolving *k*al*e*idoscopic soul.
Universal coalescence. A bird's "I" view. Wingspan.
Lifespan. Skyless, *up*aithric. **W***n*aok*w*e. Every moment,
every day, everyone gets closer to the Light from which we
all came. All the blood that ever was, is, or will be cries out
to You. Humble yourself. In order to be sound, you must
sometimes be silent.

50

Endtroduction

Let's begin at the end. At the end of the immeasrable, at the of a nanosecond, at the end of a second(s), at the end of minute(s), at the end of hour(s), at the end of the day(s), at the end of the week(s), at the end of the month(s), at the end of the year(s). At the end of life... Now, let's begin right there.

Let's begin at the *end*troduction; bordering on the margins, the periphery of eternity.

Physical death (A new "die"mension) is a thread; dimensional strings woven in linkage to the World to Come/World of Souls. The embryonic phase of the afterlife begins at physical death; as if being born/birthed into a soul transition. A fresh departure from earth and entrance into a more immaterial & discarnate realm(s). As the physical falls away, the spiritual takes center stage. The grave now home to the body (the shell of a person); the spiritual celestial ascent as it were is initialized with the soul. This soul is described by

Job as "a part of G-d," and exists both before its descent into the body and after the ascent from the body.

From the cradle of time to the grave of time and then beyond time.

Gershon Winkler explains, "Heaven and Gehinnom are spiritual places, in Judaism/Kabbalah they have no form that can be explained in physical terms. Heaven is being reunited with the Source of its energy (G-d), after completing its work/purpose. The soul has graduated and now is at peace its final reward. Gehinnom is the idea of being more distance from G-d."

Mystically speaking, Gehinnom is not a physical abode nor is Gehinnom a place for eternity, rather it's a temporary place for the soul to be cleansed. In fact it has been purported, the vast majority of souls do not stay in Gehinnom for more than eleven months. After the purification of Gehinnom, the soul enters the World to Come/Garden of Eden where it receives the rewards it earned through work in this world.

The Zohar states, "The souls must re-enter the absolute from where they have emerged. They must develop all the perfections; the germ of which is planted in them; and if they have not fulfilled this condition during one life; they must commence another... until they have acquired the condition that fits them for reunion with the Creator."

The souls that have achieved their place in the Garden of Eden will stay in their heavenly, other-worldly habitat until the time of the Resurrection of the Dead. At that time all souls will descend once again into this world to be enclothed in their resurrected shells/bodies.

It has been noted that surely the soul is capable of experiencing more when it is emancipated of a body than when it is enclothed in a physical existence. However, in order to ascend heavenly heights one must utilize the catapulting thrust of Mitzvas and Torah in this world to earn a closer ambiance to G-d. In the Mishnah, one rabbi says, "This world is like a vestibule before the World to Come. Prepare yourself in the lobby so that you may enter the resplendent banquet hall." This is based on the belief that ones station in the World to Come is determined by a merit system orbiting around one's actions in this world. What the soul experiences in the heavenly abode is a revelation of G-dliness as it is manifest in the higher realms according to the positive actions and mitzvas it accrued in this world.

The Afterlife is a very rational, natural consequence of the order of things. After all, nothing is ever lost—even the body only transforms into earth. But nothing is lost. So too, the person you are is never lost. That person—that soul—only returns to its origin. If your soul became acutely attached to the material world during its stay here, then it must painfully rip itself away to make the journey back. But if it was only a traveler, connected to its Source all along, then its ride home is heavenly, shared Rabbi Freeman.

It begins with a purpose. It ends with a purpose. Live on purpose. Learn on purpose. Love on purpose. Life and death (and everything in between) has a purpose on purpose. That's the emes (truth). The Rambam shared, Truth does not become more true by virtue of the fact that the entire world agrees with it, nor less so even if the whole world disagrees with it.

Words from the wise, and something to ponder while we're here: The real question is not whether life exists after death. The real question is whether you are alive before death. I learned that every mortal will taste death. But only some will taste life. And know, when you are born, you cry, and the world rejoices. When you die, you rejoice, and the world cries.

Learn life lessons from death. Learn death lessons from life.

Physical death is a bridge; an endtroduction to another life. A soul life. Doffing the skin of physicality and disencumbering the soul from the body introduces pulchritudinous spiritual realities of The World to Come. Hopefully we begin and open life, as well as end and close life with the proper perspectives. At least if we don't begin with the proper outlook we can always begin again each day and try to come closer to Hashem in the process. Consequently this begins to enhance our proximity to G-d which concluded at the endtroduction. For when the final curtain(s) of our eyelids descend, the ascent of our soul begins. It's been declared, every new beginning comes from some other beginning's end. This is where the beginning really starts. It starts at the end. Know, in this life, "You can't go back and change the beginning, but you can start where you are and change the ending."

Prepare...

Epilogue

Practice optimism.

About the Author

Stephen Safer spent the latter part of 13 years as the lead singer/lyricist in metal/punk rock bands spanning from his teens to late twenties. Disillusioned at times, he wanted to go beyond the notes and melodies, beyond the power chords, distortions, beats and vocals. What is beyond & outside the parameters of the auditory-emotional expression called music? What came first darkness or light? What preceded the so called Big Bang? What resides on the margins of what we know and don't know? What begins where our reality, science, philosophy, medicine, the arts and math ends?

These questions and the like propelled him to explore various avenues of spirituality within and outside of music. Here marked the genesis of his search, as his thirst and appetite for something more became piqued.

Consequently, Stephen began doing some serious soul searching around 2000/2001. He took a hiatus from music (turned off the TV and much of the distractions/ entertainment) and wanted to focus, study and delve deeper. He began perusing books on Kabbalah that he had and became increasingly more interested in the mystical elements Judaism. After dabbling in various mystical/spiritual/occult avenues (while in the bands and thereafter) he felt most drawn to the Kabbalistic teachings (albeit having minimal understanding of the aforementioned). This lead him to explore the Torah and his Judaic roots of which he was mostly unfamiliar with throughout his life. Wanting to capitalize on those proclivities he ended up selling his band equipment (PA, speakers and mics) and he purchased a plane ticket to Israel in 2000. There, he studied, learned and traveled in the Middle East for 8 months. Tuning out the static and the creature comforts of society Stephen began to find a more sincere, meaningful balance. He came back to the States with renewed vigor and a fresh perspective and appreciation for life. He struggled, but nonetheless continued on this trajectory and ultimately returned to his Jewish heritage as a result.

Presently, Stephen is married, has 3 children and practices as a clinical psychotherapist at a psychiatric inpatient hospital and has a small private practice. He continues his spiritual observance and writing as an Orthodox Jew in Savannah, GA.

His first book, *The Infinity Frequency* can be obtained through Amazon, Barnes & Noble and other online outlets. He can be contacted at npsyt@outlook.com.

CPSIA information can be obtained
at www.ICGtesting.com
Printed in the USA
LVHW011239130121
676362LV00004B/508